Antithesis

Nat   Baldwin

Published by Bridge Books, 2858 W. Belle Plaine Ave., #3, Chicago, IL,
U.S.A

bridge-books.org

ISBN: 978-1-967259-99-1
Library of Congress CIP #: 2025942941

Cover Image: Cover art: In process detail from Michael Workman, *Moloch I*, 6' x 9' oil on canvas, 2019. Volume design by Michael Workman Studio.

Notes on production: This book was typeset using Adobe Caslon Pro, Filosophia OT, Park Lane and Source Sans Pro typefaces and is printed on acid-free paper by Ingram Spark.

CONTENTS

Side B

SIDE A

Language Music

You are pretty much tempted to quit.

You are weary of pleasing authority.

It should not be a burden, it should be an opportunity, says Professor.

In 2001, applying as a transfer from School of Music, you are denied admittance to University.

Language Music consists of 12 "types" of descriptions offering a basic framework for improvisation:

> *Long tones, accented long tones, trills, staccato formings, intervallic formings, multiphonics, short attacks, angular attacks, legato formings, diatonic formings, gradient formings, subidentity formings.*

You nearly attend College instead of School of Music.

This Is Not A Novel, the 2nd book in David Markson's tetralogy, *The Notecard Quartet*, is published in 2001 by Counterpoint Press.

By combining or moving between "types," one applies *combinatory logics*.

> *I am trying now an Experiment very*
> *frequent among Modern authors;*
> *which is, to write upon Nothing.*

The epigraph to *This Is Not a Novel*, above, attributed to Swift.

After an interview with College admissions, you meet with one of the music faculty members, who utters the phrase "milk and cookies," repeatedly.

John Cage's "Lecture On Nothing" is included in *Silence*, his collection of essays and lectures published by Wesleyan University Press.

You have not read Swift.

Before moving near University after receiving rejection, the front passenger side window of your car gets smashed.

You are moving home for summer, car full of everything you own.

You watch it happen during rehearsal for the concert through a large window in the venue facing the street.

By the time you rush out he's got the whole collection, packed neatly in shoe boxes in the passenger seat.

He acknowledges the Creative Orchestra with a nod before accelerating away.

Matthew Welch (soprano, c-soprano, and alto saxophones), Phloyd Starpoli (trombone), Eli Heilbrun (tuba), Nat Baldwin (contrabass), Charlie Looker (electric guitar), Tim Keiper (percussion), Justin Yang (alto, tenor, and baritone saxophones; c-clarinet).

In the fall of 2022, your 1st semester as a student in the Graduate Program for Experimental Music/Composition, you check out from University library a CD of the concert, which lists the personnel and performance date.

This Is Not A Novel follows *Reader's Block* and precedes *Vanishing Point* and *The Last Novel.*

The narrator, Writer, uses many phrases to describe the text:

an epic poem, a sequence of cantos, a mural of sorts, an autobiography, a continued heap of riddles, a polyphonic opera of a kind, a disquisition on the maladies of the life of art, an ersatz prose alternative to The Waste Land, a treatise on the nature of man, a contemporary variant on the Egyptian Book of the Dead, an assemblage [non-linear, discontinuous, collage-like], a kind of verbal fugue, his synthetic personal Finnegans Wake, a classic tragedy

Before publication, Markson's *Wittgenstein's Mistress* is reportedly rejected 54 times.

David Foster Wallace hails it as a masterpiece—*pretty much the high point for experimental fiction in this country,* blurbs Wallace.

Ten days after handing in the manuscript for *Suicide* to his publisher, Edouard Levé dies by suicide at age 42, hanging himself.

Jessica delivers the news about the tubist, just over a year after the concert.

Levé's other books include *Autoportrait*, *Newspaper*, and *Works*, as well as 3 books of photography.

The "milk and cookies man," as he refers to himself, Charles Gayle, leaves his teaching position at College, acquired just 3 years prior, after what would have been your 1st semester.

In your 1st semester at School of Music, one professor says—*do not listen to music made past the year 1965.*

You score your 1000th point in the last game of the season, a few months before leaving for School of Music.

Anthony Braxton teaches at University from 1990 to 2013.

For Alto is credited as the 1st unaccompanied solo saxophone record.

You meet in the hallway as he walks into the venue.

Recorded in 1969, the 8 tracks approach nearly 73 minutes in duration, documenting early explorations of *Language Music* and featuring dedications to artists in each track title.

> *Ann and Peter Allen, Susan Axelrod, John Cage, Murray DePillars, Jack Gell, Leroy Jenkins, Kenny McKenny, Cecil Taylor.*

According to the CD you check out from University library, the date is May 21st, 2001.

The only names familiar to you, outside of their own references in the track listings—*John Cage, Leroy Jenkins, Cecil Taylor.*

You have not spoken since the spring of 2002.

You are familiar with all the names of collaborators with Ishmael Reed.

On August 27th, 1973, Ann Quin walks into the ocean off Palace Pier in Brighton, her body found the next day.

The epigraph of Flann O'Brien's *At Swim-Two-Birds* quotes Euripedes' *Herakles*:

> *For all things change, making way for each other.*

Three months later, her close associate and fellow British literary experimentalist B.S. Johnson slits his wrists in a bathtub.

The Free-Lance Pallbearers, Ishmael Reed's debut novel, is published in 1967, and reissued just over 3 decades later by Dalkey Archive Press.

> *I have many names. Many faces. At the moment my No. 1 X-wife and her schoolboy gigolo are following a particularity of flesh attired in a grey suit and button-down Brooks Brothers shirt.*

The 1st 3 sentences of *Tripticks*, above, Quin's last novel.

Anna Kavan's last novel *Ice* is characterized as "slipstream," a term describing a style of speculative fiction that bends genre and avoids conventional narrative.

Ishmael Reed's texts or lyrics have been performed or set to music by Albert Ayler, Billy Bang, Carla Bley, Lester Bowie, Olu Dara, Taj Mahal, David Murray, and Don Pullen, among others.

Flann O'Brien's given name is Brian O'Nolan.

Born Helen Emily Woods, Kavan originally publishes under her married name Helen Fergusen before adopting the name of the protagonist in the 2 novels she writes just prior to legally changing her name.

Other pseudonyms used by O'Brien—Myles na gCopaleen, Brother Barnabas, and George Knowall.

You have not read B.S. Johnson.

A few months later, when you move near University, a member of Creative Orchestra drops off a stack of burned CDRs, mostly Braxton, but also Giacinto Scelsi, Jo Kondo, and Karlheinz Stockhausen.

You encounter Scelsi through double bassist Joëlle Léandre and her performance of *Maknongan*, a work for solo double bass that begins the album *Okanagon*.

You encounter Cage through Léandre's interpretations of

his work on *The Wonderful Widow of Eighteen Springs*.

Cage's *Ryoanji* is written specifically for Léandre, prompted by her question to Cage:

> *Why have you never written anything for double bass?*

In the liner notes, Léandre provides 2 words for each letter of the alphabet to describe Cage, along with a short explanation regarding the choices.

> *W* *as in wood-block or week-end* > **week-end**
> *No point. He worked morning, noon and night. Like Picasso, undoubtedly. Because creating means a perpetual thrust of blood to the temples.*

Peacock Recordings, founded by Jessica Pavone, releases your 1st solo album, *Solo Contrabass*, recorded by Micah Silver, in 2003, right after you stop playing music, a period which lasts about a year.

As composers, our 1st composition is our life, says Braxton.

You begin composing this text on February 15th, 2023.

The initial working title—*This Is Not a Thesis*.

You consider writing each fragment on a notecard and collecting them in shoe box tops before assemblage.

Nothing more than a fundamentally recognizable genre all the while, says Markson.

Potential Literature

Into the silence, which was also at times a roar, of my thoughts and questions forever returning to myself to search there for an explanation of my life and its purpose, into this concentrated tiny hub of dense silent noise came the cackle of a hen from a nearby back garden, and at that moment that cackle, its distinct sharp-edged existence beneath a blue sky with white clouds, induced in me an intense awareness of freedom. The noise of the hen, which I could not even see, was an event (like a dog running or an artichoke flowering) in a field which until then had been awaiting a first event in order to become itself realisable. I knew that in that field I could listen to all sounds, all music.

An excerpt of John Berger's "Field," above, closes the 1st chapter of your contextual concert at University, the program notes of which appear in a forthcoming chapter.

Initially, you plan to include an interpretation of Antoine Beuger's *one tone. rather short. very quiet* in the performance, a duet with Parsa Ferdowsi, but ultimately decide to remove the piece from the program due to time concerns.

one tone.
rather short.
very quiet

You consider adopting a voice used in a primary section of a forthcoming chapter to the rest of the text.

once during the first half of each minute: one player plays the tone

The primary difference between the section referenced above the above fragment and the rest of the text is the omission of the word "the."

once during the second half of each minute: the other player plays the tone

You google the literary group Oulipo, a loose community of mainly French-speaking writers known for their application of formal constraints and unusual writing techniques.

sometime one player ceases to play the tone and remains silent until the end of the piece

You are currently reading, slowly and sporadically, *Species of Spaces and Other Pieces* by Georges Perec, a prominent Oulipo member.

sometime the other player ceases to play the tone and remains silent until the end of the piece

Oulipo is short for *ouvroir de littérature potentielle*, often stylized as OuLiPo, translated to English as "workshop of potential literature."

duration of the piece: at least 30 minutes

You do not find any references to texts omitting the word "the" on the Oulipo Wikipedia page.

Perec's novel *La Disparition*, published in 1969 by Gallimard, does not use the letter "e."

The 300-page work appears in English translation as *A Void* in 1994, translated by Gilbert Adair.

The exclusion of a letter within a text is a writing constraint called a lipogram.

The previous fragment is a lipogram in B, D, F, J, K, Q, V, Y, Z.

The previous fragment employs the same strategy to explain lipograms as the Oulipo Wikipedia page by referencing the lipogram in a previously written sentence.

One of the primary themes in *A Void* is its own lipogrammatic limitation.

Incurably insomniac, Anton Vowl turns on a light. According to his watch it's only 12.20. With a loud and languorous sigh Vowl sits up, stuffs a pillow at his back, draws his quilt up around his chin, picks up his whodunit and idly scans a paragraph or two; but, judging its plot impossibly difficult to follow in his condition, its vocabulary too whimsically multisyllabic for comfort, throws it away in disgust.

The opening sentences of *A Void*, above.

The translations impose the same lipogrammatic constraints adapted to their own language.

The Spanish version contains no "a," the Russian version contains no "o," the Japanese version contains no syllables using the sound "i," for example.

You realize that the word "the" contains the letter "e."

The companion work, *The Exeter Text: Jewels, Secrets, and Sex*, originally published as *Les Revenentes*, uses only one vowel, the letter "e."

Singular Pleasures by Harry Matthews, the 1st American member of Oulipo, is a collection of 61 scenes of 61 different people masturbating.

Word Events: Perspectives On Verbal Notation, edited by John Lely and James Saunders, documents a selection of text scores, including Beuger's *one tone. rather short. very quiet,* along with essays to contextualize the works.

> *[Composing is] not about creating or inventing differences or concatenations of differences, each sound is going to be different anyway.*

Raymond Queneau's *Exercises In Style* features 99 unique versions of the same story of a man witnessing an altercation on a bus.

> *I like the idea of a piece of music just being a few sounds, of performing music as just playing a few sounds.*

From the 1st episode, "Notation":

> *In the S bus, in the rush hour. A chap of about 26, felt hat with a cord instead of a ribbon, neck too long, as if someone's been having a tug-of-war with it. People getting off. The chap in question gets annoyed with one of the men standing next to him. He accuses him of jostling him every time anyone goes past. A sniveling tone which is meant to be aggressive. When he sees a vacant seat he throws himself onto it.*

Perec's *Life: A User's Manual* is dedicated to Queneau, who dies 2 years prior to its publication.

Of the living members of Oulipo, you have only read Anne F. Garreta, the 1st member to be born after the group's founding.

Beuger is a member of the composer's collective known as Wandelweiser, founded in 1992, along with Michael Pisaro-Liu, Eva-Maria Houben, Manfred Werder, and Jürg Frey, among others, known for their extreme use of silence and extended performance durations.

Garreta's debut novel *Sphinx* is the 1st work by a female member translated into English, initially published in 1986 when she is 23 years old, portraying a love story between 2 characters without giving grammatical indication of their genders.

Werder has 10 pieces that are each 4000 pages long, each lasting 533 hours and 20 minutes.

You scroll up to add an "s" to Georges Perec's name where necessary.

Each page is to last 6 minutes, while the instructional components alternate between 6 seconds of sound and 6 seconds of silence, the 1st piece of which is titled *stuck 1998*.

Pauline Oliveros' *Rock Piece* closes the introduction of your contextual concert, an example of a form of composition she calls "Sonic Meditations."

> *EACH PARTICIPANT chooses a pair of resonant rocks to use as percussive instruments.*

Other works in translation you read while composing this text—Marguerite Duras' *The Ravishing of Lol Stein*, Félix Fénéon's *Novels In Three Lines*, Jon Fosse's *The Other Name*, Patrik Ourednik's *Europeana*, Marie Redonnet's *Forever Valley*, Tiqqun's *This Is Not a Program*.

> *EACH PARTICIPANT establishes an independent pulse with the rocks.*

You try to recall the reference in a book where the author states that there was a time in their life that they thought *Life: A User's Manual* could teach them how to live and that *Suicide: A User's Manual* would teach them how to die.

> *THE PULSE is to be maintained steadily without any rhythmic interpretation or accents.*

You are nearly certain the reference is from Edouard Levé's *Autoportrait*.

> *WHILE LISTENING to the overall sound, if the participant perceives that s/he is synchronizing exactly, or in a*

simple multiple or division by 2 or 3 of another participant's pulse, s/he stops in order to listen and begin a new pulse which is independent in rate from all other pulses.

With your copy on loan, you google the above inquiry and find an excerpt from *Autoportrait* published in *The Paris Review* as "When I Look At A Strawberry, I Think of A Tongue."

When I was young, I thought Life: A User's Manual would teach me how to live and Suicide: A User's Manual how to die. I don't really listen to what people tell me. I forget things I don't like. I look down dead-end streets. The end of a trip leaves me with a sad aftertaste the same as the end of a novel. I am not afraid of what comes at the end of life. I am slow to realize when someone mistreats me, it is always so surprising: evil is somehow unreal. When I sit with bare legs on vinyl, my skin doesn't slide, it squeaks. I archive. I joke about death. I do not love myself. I do not hate myself. My rap sheet is clean. To take pictures at random goes against my nature, but since I like doing things that go against my nature, I have had to make up alibis to take pictures at random, for example, to spend three months in the United States traveling only to cities that share a name with a city in another country: Berlin, Florence, Oxford, Canton, Jericho, Stockholm, Rio, Delhi, Amsterdam, Paris, Rome, Mexico, Syracuse, Lima, Versailles, Calcutta, Bagdad.

You cut and paste the Levé text from *The Paris Review*, resize and change the font, recolor the text from grey to black, notice that Baghdad is spelled without the "h," consider adding it, leave it as it is published, insert quotes around the quoted text.

You remove the quotation marks from the Levé quote,

italicizing the text instead.

Much later in the editing process, after receiving edits for the *Sleepingfish* publication (addressed more thoroughly in a forthcoming chapter), and before you submit the manuscript to presses for publication consideration, you apply a left indent to the above quote, as well as to additional quoted material throughout the text.

The End of Oulipo? An Attempt At Exhausting a Movement consists of 2 essays—Veronica Esposito's "Eight Glances Past Georges Perec" and Lauren Elkin's "Oulipo Lite."

> *Make an effort to exhaust the subject, even if that seems grotesque, or pointless, or stupid. You still haven't looked at anything, you've merely picked out what you've long ago picked out.*

In addition to the Perec quote above, the other epigraph used for the excerpt appearing in *The New Inquiry* is from Tom McCarthy's essay on Jean-Philipe Toussaint, "Stabbing the Olive," quoted following the following fragment.

Elkin's contribution recalls the "Foulipo Manifesto" delivered by Juliana Spahr and Stephanie Young at the Noulipo Conference at Cal Arts in 2005, in which they critique "the masculinist tendencies of most constraint-based writing," while adopting Oulipian constraint techniques in the manifesto.

> *We don't want plot, depth or content: we want angles, arcs, and intervals; we want pattern. Structure is content, geometry is everything.*

In an earlier series of compositions, *calme étendue*, Beuger alternates between sound and silent phrases, with sounds expressed every 8 seconds and set within a performance duration of between 45 minutes and 9 hours.

Spahr and Young take off their clothes, put them back on and take them off again, before their voices are replaced with recordings of themselves speaking.

> *The field is a place where we experience sets of things continuously affecting one another.*

From Michael Pisaro-Liu's "Rubies Reddened By Rubies Reddening," above, an essay from which a forthcoming chapter draws its epigraph.

> *PARTICIPANTS MAY END independently, or on cue. ROCK PIECE might begin and remain out-of-doors, or move indoors. Conversely, ROCK PIECE might begin in a tight circle indoors and move out-of-doors with the participants gradually dispersing until all the pulses can no longer be heard.*

In a review of *Autoportrait*, Wayne Koestenbaum begins by defining a word you had not previously encountered—*parataxis*:

> *The placement, side by side, of two sentences whose meanings don't transparently connect.*

Slides of Color

In 2011, you encounter *HTMLGIANT—the internet literature magazine blog of the future*—founded by Blake Butler.

Action Books, Caketrain, Calamari Archive, Civil Coping Mechanisms, Dorothy, Dzanc, FC2, Featherproof, Future Tense, Lazy Fascist, Magic Helicopter, Mud Luscious, NY Tyrant, Publishing Genius, Short Flight/Long Drive, Spork, Tarpaulin Sky, Tiny Hardcore, and Two Dollar Radio are among the many small presses you explore, alongside numerous literary journals, both online and in print.

While on tour, you begin writing to writers and inviting them to shows.

You start a Tumblr page, documenting literary activity, archiving book lists, making recommendations, sharing music links and other miscellany of interest.

Of the 19 small presses listed in the fragment above the fragment above the above fragment, 6 are no longer in operation.

The 1st reading list you document and share is from 2012, listing the books you read in the order you read them:

[…]

After cutting and pasting the above list from the source, you capitalize appropriate letters, apply proper spacing between words and numbers, replace the dash between book titles and author names with "by," add translator names where necessary, and italicize book titles.

You determine the 85-book list to be too long to include in its entirely in this context, but still leave the above fragment intact after cutting the list in reference, while adding a bracketed ellipsis in its place.

At the end of the list, you include the "highlights" by category:

NOVELS: Kamby Bolongo Mean River, Slow Fade, The Dead Father, With the Animals, The Heart Is a Lonely Hunter, Ablutions, Dear Everybody, Wittgenstein's Mistress, White Noise

SHORT STORY collections: I Looked Alive, Break It Down, Windeye, AM/PM, Pee On Water, Daddy's, Fast Machine, The Collected Works of Scott McClanahan Vol. 1, Venus Drive, Big World, Knockemstiff

NOVELLAS: The Hour of the Star, The No Hellos Diet,

Ever, Autoportrait, Sylvia, Cataclysm Baby

NONFICTION: A Common Pornography, Basketball Junkie, Legs Get Led Astray, The Year of Magical Thinking

The 1st post on the page is a video clip of the book trailer for Scott McClanahan's collection *Stories V!*

The trailer features McClanahan driving on the highway lip-syncing along to Sam Cooke's *Live At the Harlem Square Club, 1963* version of "Bring It On Home to Me."

The 2nd post links to a McClanahan story published on **Everyday Genius**, and the 3rd to a review by Roxane Gay about Noëlle Revaz's *With the Animals* with the caption—*my favorite novel of 2012*.

The 4th presents a picture of basketball player Chris Herren in a red and black Fresno State uniform above a longer caption that reads:

> *Chris Herren was my hero in high school. I saw him play at an AAU tournament in Providence when I was 14. Nobody could guard him. He was fearless, he played like a fucking maniac. I wanted to play just like him. A book came out around that time called Fall River Dreams which chronicled his junior season at Durfee High in Fall River, a tough mill town in Southern Mass. It was my favorite book. At that time I only read basketball books. He had a really good college career and a brief pro career, which seemed to be cut short due to injuries. I hadn't thought about him in a while until I read an article a couple years ago saying that he crashed his car into a Dunkin' Donuts at 8am with a needle sticking out of his arm. He was shooting up heroin with his daughter in the back seat. He had*

just dropped her off at school. He died briefly and then came back to life. The last time I saw him he had a Celtics uniform on. What the fuck happened between the NBA and the Dunkin'? Last year, he came out with a memoir called Basketball Junkie and he tells us what happened. It's bonkers.

You edit the above quote by eliminating paragraph breaks, reducing the post-period space from 2 to 1, capitalizing the necessary letters, and placing an apostrophe between the "t" and "s" in the word before "bonkers."

In 2016, while you are in the process of completing an undergraduate degree in English at State University, Chris Herren is a featured speaker at an event organized by the school's athletic department in a large auditorium.

The room is packed, you and your brother are in attendance.

On the way out, you notice an audience member who spoke during the Q&A period smoking a cigarette outside the front entrance of the building.

You do not remember the question, but do remember the introduction to the question in which the audience member thanks Herren for the inspiration, mentioning that he himself is an addict, 5 years sober.

The 5th post is a video link with the caption—*Sam Pink reading some awesome shit on a train.*

Pink reads a poem called "Today I Hope A Bus Accidentally Kills Me" and has a mohawk.

A few days after the Herren event, you receive an email, along with all members of the academic community, from President, stating that a student has tragically died over the weekend.

Like you, the student was a non-traditional student, returning to school in his 30s to finish an undergraduate degree.

Majoring in Social Work, he had been working with recovering addicts, as he himself was a recovering addict, 5 years sober.

You click on the link to the obituary and look at the picture of the student.

The 6th post is a link to a story by Sam Pink called "Juliana" from the collection *Hurt Others* posted on *Muumuu House*, an online literary journal and occasional print publication edited by Tao Lin.

The 7th links to Sam Pink's book *The No Hellos Diet* with the caption:

> *I invited Sam Pink to my solo show at the Hideout in Chicago last spring. I hadn't read anything by him at the time but he seemed to be related to some folks I had just started checking out—Noah Cicero, Blake Butler, Megan Boyle. I told him to bring some of his books so I could buy them. I put him on the guestlist. He brought The No Hellos Diet, Hurt Others, and Person. Unclear whether he liked the show but he stayed the whole time, solo in the back with a hoodie. We hung out afterwards and it was awesome. Someone came up to us as we were talking and asked if we were brothers. I read the 3 books over the next couple days and loved them all. I don't know which I liked best but I read The No Hellos Diet recently*

*a second time. He has a new book, Rontel, coming out on
Valentine's Day. Sam Pink is cool.*

The 8th post reads—*great Z-BO article from GRANT-
LAND*—linking to an article on NBA player Zach
Randolph.

The 2013 year-end reading list totals 98 books.

You list the highlights again at the end, adding categories
that were not included the previous year—*IN TRANSLA-
TION* and *POETRY*.

Edouard Levé's *Suicide* begins the IN TRANSLA-
TION short list, while Ariana Reines' *Thursday* and
Dan Magers' *Partyknife* are the highlights for *POETRY*.

The only highlight in *NOVELLA* is Joanna Ruocco's *Another
Governess/The Least Blacksmith*, and Maggie Nelson's *Bluets*
begins and ends *NON-FICTION*.

There are many highlights in *NOVELS* and *SHORT
STORIES*, such as Rudy Wilson's *The Red Truck*, Eugene
Marten's *In the Blind*, Lynne Tillman's *American Genius*,
Ann Quin's *Tripticks*, Stanley Crawford's *Log of the SS the
Mrs. Unguentine*, Ken Sparling's *Dad Says He Saw You At the
Mall*, Amelia Gray's *Museum of the Weird*, Peter Markus' *The
Singing Fish*, Donald Barthelme's *Sixty Stories*, and Christine
Schutt's *Nightwork*, among others.

On October 29th, 2014, after receiving an invitation through
a social media site to exchange writing with one another,
you begin an email correspondence with Joyelle McSweeney.

Co-founder of Action Books and author of many works

across and between genres, her short story collection *Sala-mandrine: 8 Gothics* is the 83rd book you read in 2013, right after Chad Simpson's *Tell Everyone I Said Hi* and right before Jeff Jackson's *Mira Corpora*.

You were not openly writing, or sharing writing publicly, at least not under your given name, and do not remember how such an invitation could have occurred.

You share 2 pieces, one of which is titled "Portraits of a Place," an early version of what becomes "The Red Barn."

The other is your 1st publication, appearing in an online journal under a pseudonym only a few months prior to sending to McSweeney.

She responds on November 9th, 2014, providing valuable feedback and a link to Sarah Messer's "I Am the Real Jesse James."

The email thread ends on March 12th, 2015, after 20 total messages, and you do not meet in person until February 11th, 2017.

"Portraits of a Place" expands from 3 to 9 short sections after the exchange, developing the new name in the process, and is published on June 15th, 2015 in *alice blue review*, an online journal founded by Sarah and Will Gallien, the penultimate issue before ceasing operations.

"The Red Barn" is your 1st publication after abandoning the pseudonym, as well as the titular story in your 1st book, a collection of short fiction published in 2017 by Calamari Archive.

The last publication under the pseudonym is called "Ceremony," a story you consider but do not ultimately include in *The Red Barn*.

> *Eyes can't stop crossing. He said it was due to Mom's drinking. Said you came out wrong. You never had a chance to ask her. Now you're on your way to her. Boy at your side. Past the big red barn. Where it once stood tall. You tell him about how the sun set against it. About shooting hoops and shoveling snow. You don't tell him about the noise in Dad's throat. Or how you made it quit. The barn is gone is what you say. Then point to empty space. You pick the pace up. She sits just beyond the bridge. Five years to the day. Since before boy was born. The bridge covers the river. You used to lie by the shore. Broken glass all around. River sounds rushing in. Skin stuck to rocks. Boy spits over the edge. Stops to watch it drop. You imagine tossing boy off. Wonder how he would spread. You grab boy by his hand. Watch your step you tell boy. You sink in to her side. A slick mud uphill. Just a few steps left. She and boy have never met. And she is right where you left her. Cuts the same slim shape. Color sucked out. A few more cracks in the face. You're about out of breath. But now still as can be. Till boy bends down. He pulls his hand free. Brushes dirt from her name. He lies across the flat stone.*

The majority of the stories in *The Red Barn* are composed during 2 summer online workshops conducted by Peter Markus, author of *The Fish and the Not Fish*, a 150-page text composed entirely of monosyllabic words, among many others.

Markus' *The Singing Fish*, published by Calamari Archive, is the 45th book you read in 2013, right before *With Deer* by Aase Berg and right after *Trout Fishing In America* by

Richard Brautigan.

With Deer is translated by Johannes Göransson, who co-runs Action Books with McSweeney.

Ofelia Hunt's *Today & Tomorrow*, published by Magic Helicopter Press, is the 74th book you read in 2012, right before *You Private Person* by Richard Chiem and right after *By Night In Chile* by Roberto Bolaño.

Will Gallien from *alice blue* writes under various pseudonyms, including Ofelia Hunt.

After the initial release in Spanish in 2000, *By Night In Chile* is Bolaño's 1st book to be translated into English, published by New Directions in 2003.

The narrative takes place over a single night and, except for the final sentence, uses no paragraph breaks.

Blake Butler's *300,000,000* uses the structure of Bolaño's *2666*.

The book launch for *The Red Barn* takes place on April 21st, 2017 at SPACE in Portland, ME, featuring performances and videos by Annie Bielski, Mark Baumer, Claire Donato, Kafari, Lisa/Liza, Lauren Tosswill, and a live score to *Le Sang Des Betes (Blood of the Beasts)* by Patrick Carey, before you read from the book.

Blood of the Beasts is a 1949 short documentary by Georges Franju shifting between scenes of a peaceful Parisian suburb and the insides of a slaughterhouse.

The 1st scene in the film shows the shooting of a horse in the head.

A portion of the audience walks out upon sight of the activities in the slaughterhouse.

You read the closing story in the book, "Let Me See the Colts," which obliquely depicts the slaughter of horses by means of a hay bale shredder.

Before the publication of *The Red Barn*, the story is featured in the online journal *DIAGRAM* edited by Ander Monson, author of *Other Electricities*, the 53rd book you read in 2013, right after Dawn Raffel's *Further Adventures In the Restless Universe* and right before Pamela Ryder's *A Tendency To Be Gone*.

Instead of an artist bio, Monson asks you to share some context about the story's composition:

> *I wrote this story after spending a week in Amherst, MA in a workshop with Noy Holland. Who was it that said we should write what we're most afraid of? Noy really likes horses. The title is taken from a Smog song from the album A River Ain't Too Much to Love. This story is for Noy.*

Mark Baumer's contribution to the event is a video from his daily series documenting his barefoot walk across the country to raise awareness about climate change and raise money for the FANG Collective.

Exactly 3 months prior to the performance, on January 21st, 2017, Baumer is struck by an SUV and killed in Walton County, FL.

The date of his death marks 101 days into his cross-country barefoot walk.

His last words from his last video on Day 100:

Your ignorance is killing people!

In 2010, Baumer walks from Tybee Island, GA to Santa Monica, CA, wearing sneakers, in 81 days, documented in his self-published book *I Am A Road.*

You are invited to participate in a literary event in Providence together in 2016, before he leaves for his last walk, but instead plan to organize an event when he returns.

At the funeral service, you perform "A Good Day To Die," the closing track on your 2014 release *In the Hollows.*

The title track uses threads of narrative and imagery from the 2 stories that begin Breece D'J Pancake's posthumous collection, "Trilobites" and "Hollows."

Born Breece Dexter Pancake in West Virginia, only 6 of his stories are published during his lifetime.

The foreword to the collected stories begins with a short letter from Pancake's mother, Helen Pancake, and the lyrics from "Jim Dean of Indiana" by Phil Ochs.

Ochs' behavior becomes increasingly erratic after the death of his friend Víctor Jara, the Chilean protest singer and activist, murdered by the Pinochet dictatorship after the US-sponsored coup ousting democratically-elected leader Salvador Allende on September 11th, 1973.

By the mid-1970s, Ochs takes on the identity of John Butler Train, convinced that he has been murdered and that Butler Train is his replacement.

The day after the coup, Jara is detained at Estadio Chile, along with thousands of others.

Ochs hangs himself on April 9th, 1976.

Scott McClanahan and Chris Oxley, also known as the Holler Boys, also from West Virginia, make a video for "In the Hollows" upon the album's release.

On April 8th, 1979, Pancake dies of a self-inflicted gunshot wound to the head, age 26.

Blake Butler blurbs *The Red Barn*, the 1st requested and the 2nd received of the 2 solicited blurbs, delivered on February 2nd, 2017:

> *The blades, the rust, the dirt, the mouth, the meat, the blood, the sun, the glass, the skin, the word, the lake, the graves; it's a pristine and elemental form of fiction that Nat Baldwin renders, stripping language and image to its most primal animation. Like seeing slides of color pass before your face in darkness. Like remembering how to read.*

You have read *300,000,000*, but have not read *2666*.

You see Butler most recently on March 3rd, 2020, while performing in Atlanta in support of a new solo release,

AUTONOMIA: Body Without Organs.

The collection of noise-based textures and loosely-structured improvisations echo techniques developed in *Solo Contrabass*.

It feels like we froze you in a block of ice and just thawed you out because you were the superhero we needed, says Jackson Moore.

Two hours before his death, Jara asks for a notepad and writes the lyrics to his song "Estadio Chile," before it is smuggled out of the stadium.

Each track is recorded in one take, documenting a series of single, unedited performances.

> *How hard it is to sing*
> *when I must sing of horror.*
> *Horror which I am living,*
> *horror which I am dying.*

After shifting positions many times, you cut and paste the final sentence in *By Night In Chile* after the following fragment.

In 2003, Estadio Chile is renamed Estadio Víctor Jara.

> *And then the storm of shit begins.*

A Veritable Mosaic

The phrase "body without organs" is initially used by Antonin Artaud in his 1947 radio play *To Have Done With the Judgment of God*.

The 4th track on *AUTONOMIA: Body Without Organs*, "scorch atlas," takes its title from Blake Butler's 2nd book, *Scorch Atlas*, released in 2009 by Featherproof Books, the 1st Butler work you read.

Gilles Deleuze reinterprets Artaud's "body without organs" in *The Logic of Sense*, published in 1969, before expanding upon the concept in the 2 volumes of *Capitalism and Schizophrenia—Anti-Oedipus and A Thousand Plateaus*—composed in collaboration with Félix Guattari.

On February 2nd, 1948, the day before it is scheduled to air, and one month before Artaud's death, the French Radio Director cancels the broadcast.

Butler's 1st book, released earlier in 2009, is the novella *Ever* on Calamari Archive, the 43rd book you read in 2012, right after Jaime Iredell's *The Book of Freaks* and right before *The Collected Works of Scott McClanahan Vol. 1*.

The tracks "hackers" and "dark matter" come directly after "scorch atlas," named after Aase Berg books of the same titles, both translated by Johannes Göransson and published by Black Ocean.

You see Aase Berg read at Mission Creek Festival in Iowa City in 2013 before knowing who she is and leave before she finishes in order to go to another reading.

On March 9th, 2013 at the AWP Bookfair in Boston, you purchase a stack of titles from the Calamari Archive table, only months before you start writing and about 3 years before submitting *The Red Barn* manuscript to the press for publication consideration.

In 2014, at a music residency in Iowa City, facilitated by Andre Perry and Mission Creek, you do nothing but write fiction.

Autonomia: Post-Political Politics, collected accounts of the Autonomist movement in Italy originally published by Semiotext(e) as a magazine in 1980, is reissued in 2007 in a hardcover edition to begin Semiotext(e)'s Intervention Series.

The 2nd track, "the singing knives," between "body without organs" and "tripticks," takes its name from a Frank Stanford poem, also the title of his debut collection, published in 1971 and then later included in *The Light the Dead See: Selected Poems of Frank Stanford*.

Semiotexte(e) begins as a journal in 1974, founded by Sylvère Lotringer, before going on to publish full-length books under series imprint titles Active Agents, Foreign Agents, Native Agents, Intervention Series, and Animal Shelter.

In 2017, your final full year as an undergraduate, you present a multimodal project at an academic conference, initially composed in the class Writing, Rhetoric, and Emerging Technologies, featuring a triptych of digital collages layered with Berg's poem "Deer Quake," the 1st of 3 stanzas of which appear in the following fragment, along with an essay to contextualize the images and text.

> *Now the deer fever tears apart cells inside my ravaged, already*
> *so harrowed leather body. In my breath, tracks of moon wind*
> *are smarting against the throat and windpipe. I have moved*
> *around the deer, I have fastened my fibers to the hard dancing*
> *deer. Steam rose from frozen wells, ice floes chafed the channel,*
> *cold sweat broke out of the skin wall between my being*
> *and the cold. It was a hopelessly treacherous time.*

The last blurred image depicts a frozen, half-eaten deer corpse at a high level of opacity.

Frank Stanford shoots himself in the chest 3 times in his home in Fayetteville, AR on June 3rd, 1978, age 29.

His 2nd wife, Ginny Crouch Stanford, as well as the poet C.D. Wright, with whom he had cofounded Lost Roads Publishers and was having an affair, are in the house at the time of his death.

In summer 2019, at the Hewn Oaks Artist Residency in Lovell, ME, you read portions of *Autonomia: Post-Political Politics* while composing work that would become *AUTONOMIA: Body Without Organs*.

A language that looks like us, instead of trying to discipline us, says Berg.

Despite displaying "semiotext(e) intervention series 1" on the front cover, the reprint of *Autonomia* tends to be considered a prototype of the series while not actually a part of it, as subsequent releases are much shorter and formatted as 5" x 7" paperback editions following a uniform design template.

You also read at the residency, which lasts 10 days, *Ice* by Anna Kavan and *Tsunami From Solaris: Essays On Poetry* by Aase Berg.

The Battlefield Where the Moon Says I Love You, a 15,283 line epic poem, absent of stanza breaks or punctuation and published in 1978 as a 542-page book, remains Stanford's most celebrated work.

You apply to Hewn Oaks for fiction writing, but while there only compose music.

"Semiotext(e) intervention series 1" is also displayed on the front of *The Coming Insurrection* by The Invisible Committee, the nom de plume of the anonymous author, or authors, generally cited as the 1st installment in the series, published in France in 2007 and in English translation in 2009.

On November 11th, 2008 a group of 9 people in Tarnac, France are arrested and charged with sabotaging French railways, known as the Tarnac Nine.

Autonomy is the body without organs of politics, anti-hierarchic, anti-dialectic, anti-representative, says Lotringer.

You email Berg a link to the album, but hear no response.

In 1975, while a professor at Columbia University, Lotringer stages the *Schizo-Culture* conference, designed to be an intersection of post-'68 French theory with the American avant-garde.

Acker, Burroughs, Cage, Deleuze, Foucault, Guattari, Hocquenghem, and Lyotard, among others, are present at the conference.

The method of railway sabotage used by the group resembles a description in *The Coming Insurrection*, leading to the accusation that the Tarnac Nine are members of The Invisible Committee.

> *The book you hold in your hands has become the principle piece of evidence in an antiterrorism case in France directed against nine individuals who were arrested on November 11th, 2008, mostly in the village of Tarnac. They have been accused of*

"criminal association for the purposes of terrorist activity"
on the grounds that they were to have participated in the
sabotage of overhead electrical lines on France's national
roadways. Although only scant circumstantial evidence has
been presented against the nine, the French Interior Min-
ister has publicly associated them with the emergent threat
of an "ultra-left" movement, taking care to single out this
book, described as a "manual for terrorism," which they are
accused of authoring. What follows is the text of the book
preceded by the first statement of the Invisible Committee
since the arrests.

The opening of *The Coming Insurrection*, above.

I Love Dick, Chris Kraus' epistolary novel blending fiction
and memoir, written as a series of love letters to the epon-
ymous "Dick," is published by Semiotext(e) in 1997.

One of the 9 people arrested, Julien Coupat, is the founder of
the anarchist philosophical journal Tiqqun, which produces
2 issues in 1999 and 2001.

Nanni Balestrini's novel *The Unseen* is originally published
in 1987, the English translation by Liz Heron appearing in
1989 through Verso Books, while the updated 2011 edition
features a foreword by Antonio Negri.

Tiqqun's articles are written anonymously.

In 2017, Kraus publishes *Acker On Acker*, a biography on
Kathy Acker, on Semiotext(e).

The Red Brigades kidnap former Italian prime minister and

Christian Democrat leader Aldo Moro in March of 1978, holding him hostage for 45 days, before calling Moro's wife to inform her of her husband's imminent death, recording and broadcasting the conversation on television.

Of the 2 issues published by Tiqqun, 4 books have appeared in English translation as part of the Intervention Series.

Balestrini, an active participant in the Autonomist movement, founded the experimental writing group Neoavanguardia with Umberto Eco, among others, also known as Gruppo 63.

Cage and Deleuze present their work at *Schizo-Culture* together—Deleuze offers an early articulation of the concept of the "rhizome" before it appears as an integral part of *A Thousand Plateaus*, while Cage performs *Empty Words*, a fragmented encounter with Thoreau's *Journal* through *I Ching* chance operations.

Coupat sets up a commune in 2005 in the village of Tarnac where he and his friends run a farm and an all-purpose store.

Balestrini's novel *Tristano* claims to be one of 109,027,350,432,000 possible variations of the same work of fiction, paragraphs reorganized for each published copy, the English translation individually numbered, starting from 10,000 (running sequentially from the Italian and German editions).

Preliminary Materials For Theory of the Young-Girl, the 3rd release by Tiqqun on Semiotext(e), is translated by Ariana Reines.

Antonio Negri is wrongly accused of making the phone call and being the "mastermind" behind the Red Brigades before fleeing to France.

When the disruptive crowd states they can't hear the unamplified Cage over the chaos, he responds—*you can, if you listen.*

Negri eventually returns to Italy after a plea bargain agreement for a reduced sentence where he serves out the remainder of his term, during which many of his most influential works are published.

The Unseen uses virtually all lowercase letters and no punctuation.

The opening paragraph in *Autonomia: Post-Political Politics* by translator John Johnston, introducing the introduction by Lotringer, "In the Shadows of the Red Brigades":

> *In the summer of 1979, Sylvère Lotringer traveled to Italy to meet with members of Autonomia (etym. "self-ruled"), a cultural, post-Marxist left-wing political movement that had come to involve tens of thousands people. Aptly described by their merciless prosecutor as "a veritable mosaic made of different fragments, a gallery of overlapping images, of circles and collectives without any social organization," Autonomia was comprised almost equally of intellectuals and young workers and unemployed youth. Opposed to work ethics and hierarchy as much as exclusively ideological rigidity, they invented their own forms of social "war-fair"—pranks, squats, collective reappropriations (pilfering), self-reductions (rent, electricity, etc.), pirate*

radios, sign tinkering—extending the spirit of May '68 over a broad social landscape. In the summer of 1977, the assassination of a young autonomist by a neo-fascist in Rome triggered massive autonomist demonstrations throughout Italy, and it seemed for a while that the Movement would take over the entire country. ("I didn't know what we would have done with it," subsequently quipped Franco Piperno, one of their leaders. Autonomists were not interested in seizing power.)

Balestrini's *We Want Everything* centers around the factory wildcat strikes that set off the Hot Autumn of 1969, the beginning of the Years of Lead.

The 2022 Verso edition features an introduction by Rachel Kushner.

You briefly meet Kushner at the Mission Creek Festival in 2014 after she reads from *The Flamethrowers*, a novel set in New York City and Italy in the 1970s.

She signs your recently purchased copy of her book, which you do not read until 2020.

Schizo-Culture: The Event, the Book combines the original issue of the journal with previously unpublished materials and a comprehensive record of the conference, published in its expanded form in 2014.

In addition to frequent references to the Red Brigades in the novel, Kushner also mentions The Motherfuckers, an anarchist affinity group that grew out of the Dada-influenced art group Black Mask, which started in 1966 and produced a broadside of the same name.

Hot Autumn is followed by the Piazza Fontana bombing in December 1969 in Milan, killing 17 and injuring 88, carried out by the fascist paramilitary group Ordine Nuovo and their collaborators.

Nine days after the phone call, the government still unwilling to cooperate with the Red Brigades, Aldo Moro is put in the trunk of a car, covered in a blanket, and shot 10 times.

After the bombing is attributed to anarchists, precisely the intent of the Strategy of Tension, over 80 arrests were made, including Guiseppe Pinelli, an anarchist railway worker, who falls or jumps or is thrown to his death from a 4th-floor window while under police interrogation.

The commissioner involved in the interrogation, Luigi Calabresi, is murdered by members of Lotta Continua in revenge.

Accidental Death of An Anarchist, a play by Dario Fo based on the Piazza Fontana bombing, premiers in 1970.

In May 1968, Black Mask goes underground and changes its name to Up Against the Wall Motherfuckers, often shortened to The Motherfuckers, taken from the Amiri Baraka poem "Black People!":

> *The magic words are: Up against the wall, mother fucker, this is a stick up!*

Patty Hearst famously shouts the line during the robbery of Hibernia Bank in San Francisco.

> *'77 wasn't like '68. '68 was anti–establishment, '77 was radically alternative. This is why the "official" version portrays '68 as good and '77 as bad; in fact, '68 was co-opted whereas '77 was annihilated. This is why, unlike '68, '77 could never make for an easy object of celebration.*

The epigraph to "Creeping May Versus Triumphant May" in Tiqqun's *This Is Not a Program*, above, attributed to Nanni Balestrini and Primo Moroni.

Balestrini dies on May 19th, 2019, at age 83.

The acceptance of death is the source of all life, says Cage.

Floating Gardens

The Weather Underground forms the May 19th Communist Organization, also known as May 19 Coalition, May 19
Communist Coalition, and M19CO, in 1978.

Known at the time as LeRoi Jones, Amiri Baraka co-authors
a "Declaration of Conscience" in 1961 with Diane di Prima,
Elaine de Kooning, and Lawrence Ferlinghetti, among others,
in support of Fidel Castro and the Cuban Revolution.

A combination of members of the Weather Underground
and the Black Liberation Army, the coalition also includes
members of the Black Panthers, White Panthers, and Republic
of New Afrika.

Di Prima, whose grandfather Domenico Mallozzi is an activist
associated with anarchists Emma Goldman and Carlo Tresca,
begins writing *Revolutionary Letters* in 1968, publishing the 1st
of 4 versions 3 years later on Ferlinghetti's Pocket Poet Series.

Baraka is a member of The Umbra Poets Workshop, along with Ishmael Reed, Archie Shepp, and Cecil Taylor, among others.

In 1964, composer and trumpeter Bill Dixon organizes the October Revolution In Jazz festival at the Cellar Cafe in NYC.

Free Jazz Communism: Archie Shepp-Bill Dixon Quartet at the 8th World Festival of Youth and Students in Helsinki 1962 is published in 2020 by Rab-Rab Press, featuring contributions from Angela Davis, Perry Robinson, and Shepp, among others.

The composition referenced in the fragment following the following fragment uses quotations from the Italian traditional socialist song "Bandiera Rossa," as well as "Solidarity Song" by Bertolt Brecht and Hanns Eisler.

Baraka and di Prima co-edit the small magazine *The Floating Bear*, publishing 25 issues in the early 1960s.

Ursula Oppens premiers *The People United Will Never Be Defeated!* in 1976, a solo piano work by Frederic Rzewski based on a set of 36 variations on the Chilean song "¡El pueblo unido jamás será vencido!" by Sergio Ortega and Quilapayún.

The October Revolution In Jazz is organized in parallel with the development of the Jazz Composer's Guild, a short-lived but influential musician's cooperative founded by Dixon alongside Carla Bley, Sun Ra, Archie Shepp, and Cecil Taylor, among others.

With over 18,000 people attending from 137 countries, The 8th World Festival is organized by the World Federation of Democratic Youth and the International Union of Students, whose motto is—*For Peace and Friendship*.

Taylor operates the mimeograph machine for *The Floating Bear* in di Prima's East Village apartment.

Liberation Music Orchestra, Charlie Haden's debut as a leader, features "Songs of the United Front" by Bertolt Brecht and Hanns Eisler, "War Orphans" by Ornette Coleman, 3 Spanish folks songs popularized during the Spanish Civil War and arranged by Carla Bley, and "Song For Ché" by Haden.

Our vindication will be black as the color of suffering is black, as Fidel is black, as Ho Chi Minh is black, says Shepp.

"An Artist Speaks Bluntly," originally published in *DownBeat* in 1965, is the 1st of 3 Shepp texts reprinted in *Free Jazz Communism*.

After the US Postal Service seizes *The Floating Bear #9*, the FBI charges the editors with obscenity for publishing the William S. Burroughs piece "Roosevelt After the Inauguration."

Grove Press delays the publication of *Naked Lunch* over the controversy.

If my music doesn't suffice, I will write you a poem, a play.

Shepp writes the play *The Communist* in the early 1960s, which he is forced to rename *Junebug Graduates Tonight*.

The debut performance for the Feminist Improvising Group (FIG), founded by bassoonist Lindsay Cooper and vocalist Maggie Nichols, occurs in 1977 at the Music For Socialism festival in London at the Almost Free Theatre.

The 1st version of the group Iskra 1903, featuring Derek Bailey, Barry Guy, and Paul Rutherford, releases their self-titled debut in 1972 on Bailey's Incus Records, a label co-founded with Tony Oxley and Evan Parker.

One of many offshoots of FIG, Cooper and Nichols form a trio with double bassist Joëlle Léandre, releasing *Live At the Bastille* in 1982, before multiple albums appear in the 1990s and 2000s under the name Les Diaboliques.

In many Slavic languages, "iskra" translates to "spark."

Léandre and Nichols are also part of pianist Irène Schweizer's 1988 release *The Storming of the Winter Palace*, with George Lewis and Günter Sommer.

The quote following the following fragment ends an earlier draft of this chapter, previously titled "Spark."

The motto for the Russian underground newspaper, *Iskra*, founded and managed by Vladimir Lenin from 1900-1903, comes from a line Alexander Odoevsky writes in response to a poem by Alexander Pushkin:

> *From a spark a fire will flare up.*

Two days after the assassination of Fred Hampton, deputy chairman of the Black Panther Party, the Weather

Underground goes on a bombing spree in Chicago, destroying numerous police vehicles.

Val Wilmer's *As Serious As Your Life: Black Music and the Free Jazz Revolution, 1957-1977* is originally published by Allison and Busby in 1977 and then reissued by Serpent's Tail in 2018, the title referencing a quote from McCoy Tyner:

Music's not a plaything; it's as serious as your life.

The October Revolution In Jazz marks the inaugural performance for the New York Art Quartet, the original lineup featuring Milford Graves, Roswell Rudd, John Tchicai, and Lewis Worrell, the latter soon replaced by Reggie Workman.

Amiri Baraka appears on "Black Dada Nihilismus," the 2nd track on the group's self-titled debut released in 1965 on ESP-Disk.

During the recording, Graves cannot hear Baraka and attempts to read his lips.

Percussion Ensemble appears the following year on ESP-Disk, Graves' debut as a leader, a duo with Sonny Morgan featuring 5 tracks titled "Nothing 5-7," "Nothing 11-10," "Nothing 19," "Nothing 13," and "Nothing."

Homage to Leroi Jones & Other Early Works presents previously unpublished "exercises," correspondences, and diary excerpts from Kathy Acker, appearing nearly 2 decades after her death on Lost and Found.

Hampton's bodyguard, William O'Neal, a police informant,

outlines a detailed map of the Hampton residence for the FBI and Chicago police, who fire over 100 rounds of ammunition into the apartment on the morning of December 4th, 1969, killing Hampton immediately, 21 at the time.

Archie Shepp's *Fire Music*, released in 1965 on Impulse! Records, features the track "Malcolm, Malcolm Semper Malcolm."

Malcolm X, previously known as Malcolm Little and then el-Hajj Malik el-Shabazz, is born on May 19th, 1925.

Cecil Taylor's prose poem "Sound Structure of Subculture Becoming Major Breath/Naked Fire Gesture" appears as the liner notes to *Unit Structures*, recorded on May 19th, 1966 and released later that year on Blue Note Records.

The first time I heard about Malcolm X, it was from Cecil Taylor, says Shepp.

Taylor's 1st published poems—"Scroll No. 1" and "Scroll No. 2"—appear in the short-lived jazz magazine *Sounds and Fury*, which are reprinted in the liner notes to *Indent*, a solo album released in 1973 on Taylor's own Unit Core Records before being reissued by Freedom Records.

> *Justice invisibly*
> *impenetrable*
> *lighted masks*
> *calcimined mimes*
> *ejaculate polyglot*
> *systoles*
> *Dry cell of money*

has locked the minds
and cauterized hearts

Long-time Taylor collaborator Jimmy Lyons releases his debut as a leader, *Other Afternoons*, in 1969 on BYG as part of their Actuel series, one of many recording sessions produced in Paris following the Pan-African Cultural Festival in Algiers.

The session also generates albums by the Art Ensemble of Chicago, Andrew Cyrille, Sunny Murray, Archie Shepp, Alan Silva, and Clifford Thornton, among others.

Thornton's debut as a leader, *Freedom & Unity*, appears in 1969 on Third World Records, with the opening track "Free Huey" dedicated to Huey P. Newton, founder of the Black Panther Party.

William O'Neal is interviewed for part 2 of *Eyes On the Prize*, a 14-part documentary series about the Civil Rights Movement, regarding his infiltration of the Black Panther Party and his role in the execution of Fred Hampton.

In *Blood and Guts in High School*, Kathy Acker uses cut-up techniques popularized by Burroughs, as well as forms of collage, inserting letters, poems, drama scenes, dream visions and drawings into the work, while incorporating text from her previous publication "Hello, I'm Erica Jong."

On the night the opening episode airs, O'Neal commits suicide by running into street traffic.

The Childlike Life of the Black Tarantula: Some Lives of Murderesses, Acker's debut novel, appears in 1973 under the pseudonym Black Tarantula.

Twenty-five days after witnessing her fiancee's murder, Akua Njeri, at the time known as Deborah Johnson, gives birth to their son, Alfred Johnson, whose name she legally changes to Fred Hampton Jr. when he turns 10.

Acker freely admits to using plagiarism in her work.

Njeri attends O'Neal's funeral, but does not follow through on her intention to spit in and turn over the casket.

> *Without language the only thing the rebels can kill are themselves.*

Ishmael Reed reads from *The Free-Lance Pallbearers* prior to its publication on the compilation *East Village Other*, released on ESP-Disk in 1966.

Other artists appearing on the comp include Marion Brown, Allen Ginsberg, Ronald Shannon Jackson, Tuli Kupferberg of The Fugs, Gerard Malanga, Peter Orlovsky, Ingrid Superstar, The Velvet Underground, and Steve Weber of the Holy Modal Rounders.

The recording captures a live radio report of First Daughter Luci Baines Johnson's wedding, while the press blurb notes that the date falls on the 21st anniversary of Hiroshima.

> *I live in HARRY SAM. HARRY SAM is something else. A big not-to-be-believed out-of-sight, sometimes referred to as O-BOP-SHE-BANG or KLANG-A-LANG-A-DING-DONG. SAM has not been seen since the day thirty years ago when he disappeared into the John with a weird ravaging illness.*

The opening paragraph of *The Free-Lance Pallbearers*, above.

Under the personnel listing, Andy Warhol is credited with "silence," as he was reportedly present during the recording session, watching and listening, silently.

One of the last releases in the original ESP-Disk catalog is Frank Lowe's debut as a leader, *Black Beings*, highlighting 4 live sets performed by Lowe's quintet over 2 nights at Artists House, Ornette Coleman's loft space, in 1973, also marking double bassist William Parker's recording debut, 21 at the time.

Double bassist Fred Hopkins, known for his work in the trio Air, with Steve McCall and Henry Threadgill, appears on each of the 5 *Wildflowers: The New York Loft Jazz Sessions* releases, a series documenting 10 days of performances in May 1976 at Studio Rivbea, a loft venue run by Sam and Beatrice Rivers.

In addition to Parker, Lowe's group features saxophonist Joseph Jarman, drummer Rashad Sinan, and a violinist listed as The Wizard.

Forming in 1971, Air initially calls themselves Reflection, before changing their name after relocating from Chicago to NYC in 1975.

The Revolutionary Ensemble, a trio featuring drummer Jerome Cooper, violinist Leroy Jenkins, and double bassist Sirone, releases their debut *Vietnam* in 1972 on ESP-Disk, documenting a live performance at Washington Square Methodist Church, also known as Peace Church, earlier that year.

Air releases 11 albums between 1975-1986, including *Air Song, Open Air Suit, Air Time, Live Air*, and *Air Mail*, many appearing on the Italian label Black Saint.

The Creative Construction Company releases 2 albums on Muse Records in the mid-1970s, after the group had already disbanded, the 1st reissued as *Muhal* on the Italian label Vedette, both consisting of live material from a Peace Church performance on May 19th, 1970.

In an earlier draft of this chapter, at the time titled "Coagulated Verbosity," the footnote to the above fragment reads:

> *Often shortened to CCC, the group features Muhal Richard Abrams, Anthony Braxton, Richard Davis, Leroy Jenkins, Steve McCall, and Wadada Leo Smith.*

Jenkins appears on Anthony Braxton's debut as a leader, *3 Compositions of New Jazz*, released in 1968 on Delmark Records, alongside Wadada Leo Smith and AACM co-founder Muhal Richard Abrams.

The opening 2 tracks are graphically titled and credited to Braxton, roughly translated as "(840m)-Realize-44M-44M (Composition 6 E)" and "N-M488-44M-Z (Composition 6 D)," while the closer, "The Bell," is credited to Smith.

The closing track on *Air Mail* is "C.T., J.L.," dedicated to Cecil Taylor and Jimmy Lyons.

Roscoe Mitchell's debut *Sound* appears on Delmark in 1966, the 1st release from an AACM member after its founding the previous year, leading briefly to the formation of the Roscoe Mitchell Art Ensemble and then ultimately to the Art Ensemble of Chicago, the core lineup around Mitchell in place by 1969 with Lester Bowie, Malachi Favors, Joseph Jarman, and Don Moye.

Initially, The Wizard is believed by many to be Leroy Jenkins.

Braxton's *Silence* is released in 1975 on Freedom Records, a trio with Jenkins and Smith.

Co-founder of the Black Artists Group (BAG) in St. Louis, Julius Hemphill appears on Braxton's *New York, Fall 1974* before founding the World Saxophone Quartet.

Violinist Billy Bang appears on William Parker's debut as a leader, *Through Acceptance of the Mystery Peace*, released initially on Parker's Centering label in 1980 before a reissue appears in expanded form on Eremite Records in 1998.

According to Parker's liner notes, the title comes from a line in a poem by Kenneth Patchen:

> *Through acceptance of the mystery peace & only through peace can come acceptance of the mystery.*

Bang releases nearly 30 albums as a leader, including *Vietnam: The Aftermath* and *Vietnam: Reflections*, the former featuring the track "Yo! Ho Chi Minh Is In the House."

Patchen collaborates with John Cage in 1942 on the radio play *The City Wears A Slouch Hat*, while reportedly working with Charles Mingus in the 1950s, though no known recorded documentation of the latter collaboration exists.

Before being reissued by Freedom, Hemphill's debut *Dogon A.D.* is released in 1972 on his own Mbari Records.

Adopting the name during the Vietnamese independence

movement in the mid-1940s, Ho Chi Minh combines a common Vietnamese surname with a given name meaning "bright spirit" or "clear will."

He uses between 50 and 200 pseudonyms, reportedly, before coming to power.

In addition to "Spark" and "Coagulated Verbosity," earlier drafts of this chapter are titled "Bright Spirit, Clear Will."

It is later revealed that The Wizard is Raymond Lee Cheng.

Hemphill's *Raw Materials and Residuals*, a trio with Abdul Wadud and Don Moye, appears in 1978 on Black Saint.

Ho Chi Minh is born on May 19th, 1890.

Peter Brötzmann's *Machine Gun* is released in May 1968 on his own BRÖ label, the reissue appearing 3 years later on FMP.

The above follows his debut *For Adolphe Sax* and precedes *Nipples*, while the album title references a nickname given to Brötzmann by Don Cherry.

All 3 albums referenced in the above fragment feature Peter Kowald on double bass.

Three decades later, Brötzmann releases *The Chicago Octet/ Tentet* on Okka Disk, half of the tracks recorded live at the Empty Bottle in Chicago over 2 performances.

The liner notes by John Corbett begin and end with quotes

from Dada artist Tristan Tzara.

> *To live without pretension, to dance on iron spikes, telegraphically, or to keep quiet on the equinoctial line, to know that at every instant—perpetua mobilia—it is today.*

In 1984, Kowald organizes the Sound Unity Festival in NYC, in collaboration with William Parker and Patricia Nicholson, a precursor to the Vision Festival, which includes performances by Rashied Ali, Billy Bang, Peter Brötzmann, Don Cherry, Marilyn Crispell, Charles Gayle, Jeanne Lee, Frank Lowe, Jemeel Moondoc, Irène Schweizer, David S. Ware, and Frank Wright, among others, documented in the film *Rising Tones Cross*.

Charles Gayle releases his debut *Always Born* just before he turns 50, going on to release 36 albums as a leader, including *Repent, Touchin' On Trane, Consecration*, and *Kingdom Come*.

A member of Anthony Braxton's quartet from 1983-1995, Marilyn Crispell's quartet release *Live In Berlin*, with Billy Bang, John Betsch, and Peter Kowald, appears on Black Saint in 1984.

Gayle and Kowald are featured heavily in the film, both in performance and in conversation with one another, though no other known recorded documentation of their collaborations exist.

One of the earliest documents of her solo piano music, *Pianosolo—A Concert In Berlin*, is released the previous year on FMP.

Was Da Ist, Kowald's solo debut, appears on FMP in 1994,

featuring 23 tracks clocking just over 72 minutes, the album title translating to "what is there."

Gayle also appears on work by Sunny Murray, William Parker, the Sirone Bang Ensemble, Henry Rollins, and Cecil Taylor.

Kowald's *Duos: Europa-America-Japan* features improvisations with different collaborators on each of the 37 tracks, opening with a double bass duet with Joëlle Léandre.

What is there is quite a lot, actually almost everything.

Historic Music Past Tense Future documents a live performance by Peter Brötzmann, Milford Graves, and William Parker in 2002, appearing on Black Editions Archive 2 decades later, the label's inaugural release in a series presenting previously unreleased work by Graves.

After the death of Jimmy Lyons (on May 19th, 1986), Cecil Taylor forms a trio with William Parker and Tony Oxley, releasing *Looking (Berlin Version) The Feel Trio* on FMP in 1990.

Fred Moten's poetry collection *The Feel Trio* is a finalist for the 2014 National Book Award.

A feature-length portrait of Graves, directed by Jake Meginsky and co-directed by Neil 'Cloaca' Young, is released in 2018—*Milford Graves Full Mantis.*

After being presented a Lifetime Achievement Award, Léandre performs with Moten at the 2023 Vision Festival.

At the opening of EMPAC in Troy, NY in 2008, Taylor performs with Pauline Oliveros, documented on the DVD *Solo. Duo. Poetry*, which closes with a 75-minute reading—*Floating Gardens: The Poetry of Cecil Taylor*.

> *A poetry... that is of the music; a poetry that would articulate the music's construction; a poetry that would mark and question the idiomatic difference that is the space-time of performance, ritual, and event; a poetry, finally, that becomes music in that it iconically presents those organizational principles that are the essence of music.*

The documentary *Imagine the Sound* features extensive interviews and performances by Paul Bley, Bill Dixon, Archie Shepp, and Cecil Taylor.

Moten's essay, "Sound In Florescence (Cecil Taylor Floating Garden)," quoted above the above fragment, appears in his debut book, *In the Break: The Aesthetics of the Black Radical Tradition*.

In September 2023, as an artist-in-residence at Wave Farm, percussionist and composer Susie Ibarra, a former student of Graves' whose collaborators include Pauline Oliveros, William Parker, Wadada Leo Smith, and David S. Ware, among many others, creates a series of sonic sculptures and sonic habitats called *Floating Gardens*.

It seems to me what music is, is… everything that you do, says Taylor.

The Story That Most Spends You

Acker, a lyric essay written through Kathy Acker's prose, public statements, and private archives, by Douglas A. Martin, the Associate Director of Creative Writing at University, is released in 2017 on Nightboat Books.

You write to Martin, as well as Associate Professor of English Danielle Vogel, author of *A Library of Light*, among others, with the subject line "Writing Tutuorial," discovering the typo just after sending at 1:34 am on May 11th, 2023:

> *Dear Danielle and Douglas,*
>
> *My name is Nat Baldwin and I'm a graduate student at […] in the Experimental Music/Composition program. I'm reaching out to see if either of you would be interested in doing a writing tutorial with me in the fall. My thesis—Antithesis—is a fragmented, hybrid text, a collage of memories and*

encounters exploring shifts in voice via program notes, field recording journals, open(text) scores, this email(?), and an annoying amount of self-reflexive material (the narrator narrates when and where edits are made). It began as a direct reference to Markson's Notecard Quartet and has since moved in many directions.

Music has taken priority in recent years, but I've done writing workshops in the past with Peter Markus and Noy Holland, used to organize a ton of literary events, and released a book of short fiction called The Red Barn on Calamari Archive in 2017. I'm super excited to explore new formal territory (for me) and to return to writing within this context. I'd be honored to work with either of you if you have the time and interest. The only proper class offered in the fall that could possibly work in my schedule would be the Senior Writing Seminar, which I'd be happy to take if the tutorial idea is not an option. Thank you both so much for reading and considering!

All my best,
nat

The primary literary event you are referring to above is a series you curate as part of Waking Windows, a multidisciplinary arts festival in Portland, ME, from 2015-2019.

The inaugural lineup, in order of appearance:

12pm—Blue
Henry Finch
Catie Hannigan
Tim Horvath

Jessica Anthony
Colin Winnette

1pm—The Bearded Lady's Jewel Box
Niles Baldwin
Michele Christle
Jensen Beach
Juliet Escoria
Scott McClanahan

2pm—Tandem Coffee
meg willing
Douglas W. Milliken
Gregory Howard
Sarah Gerard
Ottessa Moshfegh

The 1st book you read on summer break from University is the memoir *Rerun Era* by Joanna Howard, an uncorrected proof given to you by the book's editor Rita Bullwinkel, author of the short story collection *Belly Up* and the novel *Headshot*.

When William S. Burroughs shoots his wife Joan Vollmer in the head, a drunken game of William Tell, according to reports, their son William S. Burroughs Jr, age 4, is in the room.

At a book release celebration for *Headshot* in Providence, RI, on March 17th, 2024, at Twenty Stories, you perform your song "Knockout" to begin the event.

Howard's acknowledgements at the end of the book include "great thanks and love to Renee Gladman, Danielle Vogel, Jen Bervin, and Joanna Ruocco for their constant and continued support."

William S. Burroughs Jr., also known as Billy Burroughs or William Seward Burroughs III, writes 3 novels, 2 of which are published before his death at age 33 of cirrhosis of the liver.

Other writers featured at the festival in subsequent years include Noah Burton, Tobias Carroll, Carolyn Chute, Annie DeWitt, Sarah Rose Etter, Kristen Ghodsee, Meghan Gilliss, Myronn Hardy, Noy Holland, Robert Lopez, Peter Markus, Sam Michel, Katy Mongeau, Andre Perry, Amy Sauber, and Roy Scranton, among many others.

One of the 1st events you attend at University is an art show featuring work by Renee Gladman, which includes the piece *Untitled Score (orange yellow), pastel and ink on paper, 2020* used for the album cover on the 2022 self-titled release from Gerald Cleaver, Brandon Lopez, and Fred Moten.

David Ohle, author of the post-apocalyptic cult classic *Motorman*, originally published in 1972 and out of print for over 30 years before being reissued by 3rd Bed in 2004 and then Calamari Archive in 2008, edits William S. Burroughs Jr's posthumous work, *Cursed From Birth: The Short, Unhappy Life of William S. Burroughs, Jr.*, blending parts of an unfinished novel, *Prakriti Junction*, with journals, poems, correspondences and conversations.

In 2016, you curate a collection of prose and poems for Dostoyevsky Wannabe, a UK-based small press, the 3rd installment of their Sampler series, *Cassette 68*.

Side A: Katy Mongeau, Timothy Willis Sanders, Sean Kilpatrick, B.B.P Hosmillo

Side B: Julie Reverb, Paul Cunningham, Rita Bullwinkel, Vanessa Angelica Villarreal

Renee Gladman's *Event Factory* is the 63rd book you read in 2013, the inaugural release by Dorothy, a publishing project, co-founded by Danielle Dutton, author of *Sprawl*, among others, the 30th book listed on your 2014 reading log, one of the last posts shared on your Tumblr page.

> *But it's to me this evening something has to happen, to my body as in myth and metamorphosis, this old body to which nothing ever happened, or so little, which never met with anything, wished for anything, in its tarnished universe, except for the mirror to shatter, the plane, the curved, the magnifying, the minifying, and to vanish in the havoc of its images.*

The epigraph to *Event Factory*, above, from Samuel Beckett.

Each chapter in *Cursed From Birth* ends in commentary from other writers, including Burroughs, Sr., Allen Ginsberg, and Anne Waldman.

The Basketball Article, a collaborative work by Waldman and Bernadette Mayer, written as a magazine assignment that is ultimately rejected for being "too technical" and then "not technical enough," is originally published in an edition of 100 by Angel Hair Books in 1975.

The front cover features a photo of Bill Walton being questioned at a press conference, with Micki Scott, wife of political activist Jack Scott, looking on.

> *Somebody says to us, "There are too many basketball players." Then somebody says, "There are too many poets." We imagine a*

great conference of poets with trainers, doctors and coaches, keeping them in fine physical and mental shape. We wonder what their work would be like. Attendance, 20,239. The poets would perform in gym suits, showing their long lean legs and muscular shoulders. The older poets comment on the game or go into business. One poet is the center, there are two forwards and two guards, but anyone can score. The center, generally, must simply try to get the words away from the opposing teams of poets and the guards bring them downcourt to be used. The referees can be cursed at during and after the game. Some poets are booed for using the language awkwardly, others cheered for coming up with a new style of play. Most of the coaches are former players who continue to read and write books. A foul is called on any poet who deliberately deranges the language. A poet in a state of ecstasy makes a 3-point play. Fouled in the act of writing by personal insults, the poet would go to the line.

While living with Walton, Scott provides refuge for Patty Hearst and other members of the Symbionese Liberation Army as they evade the FBI, driving them across the country in disguise.

On May 23rd, 2008, before readings by featured writers Brian Evenson and David Ohle, you perform a solo set as part of the Littoral series at ISSUE Project Room in Brooklyn, curated by the venue's founder Suzanne Fiol.

At the time, you had not heard of Evenson or Ohle, or read any contemporary or experimental fiction, nearly turning down the offer for the show, a long drive from home in Maine.

After controversy over the depictions of violence in his debut collection of stories *Altmann's Tongue*, published in 1994 by Knopf, Evenson resigns from his teaching position at Brigham Young University, formally leaving the Mormon Church in 2000.

Ohle, a pallbearer at William S. Burroughs funeral, releases both *Boons & the Camp* and *The Blast* through Calamari Archive after the *Motorman* reissue.

Altmann's Tongue is reissued by University of Nebraska Press, also known as Bison Books, in 2002, adding an introduction by philosopher Alphonso Lingis and including the O. Henry Prize winning story "Two Brothers," originally published in *Contagion*.

Evenson blurbs Noy Holland's short story collection *Swim For the Little One First*, which appears on FC2 in 2012.

> *In wonderfully cadenced and concise prose, Swim For the Little One First cracks the chest of struggling lives to show the hearts beating within. These stories of difficulty are not sentimental, nor are they artificially cold: they are wonderfully, nakedly human.*

In 2014, you and Evenson participate in the Mission Creek Festival in Iowa City.

The opening story in *The Red Barn*—"A Crack In the Back of the Barn"—is composed during a week-long workshop with Holland in 2016 in Amherst, MA.

> *I watch through a crack in the back of the barn. The sound*

tears up from the gut through the throat. They say it is the stress before the sound that taints the quality of meat. The blade sticks beneath fatty pockets of the face. When handle meets skin the body gets stuck. The cut runs down the throat to the chest. The knife must not twist. They hold the weight down to drain the blood out. If they step too close to the kicks a leg bone can break. I have seen a shin split clean in two. They cut the tendons running through the center of the hooves. These they fasten with a chain and hook. They drag it then to the barrel where scalding water waits. The water must not reach a boil. They hoist the body up. Rising steam meets the carcass where it hangs. The body, in the sun, all muscle and meat.

You read the story to begin a solo set in Amherst, MA in 2017, with Holland in the audience, on a bill with the Travis Laplante-led saxophone quartet Battle Trance (featuring Patrick Breiner, Matt Nelson, and Jeremy Viner), organized by Jake Lichter at a venue on a college campus called The Red Barn.

The 1st of 3 short sections of the story, above the above fragment.

One of Evenson's former students, Joanna Ruocco, contributes the 2nd requested and 1st received blurb for *The Red Barn*:

> *In The Red Barn, Nat Baldwin decomposes narrative's safe spaces. The symbols in the nightmare landscape are nothing other than themselves. Nails. Boards. Tubs. Chains. Buckets. Teeth. A story of boys is stripped sentence by sentence. What's left is the brutal music of language laid bare.*

You consider Ruocco's diptych *Another Governess/The Least Blacksmith*, which won the FC2 Catherine Doctorow

Innovative Fiction Prize in 2012, judged by Ben Marcus, to be the most directly influential work on *The Red Barn*, most specifically the latter title.

You initially write to her on December 16th, 2016, at 12:38 pm.

Hi Joanna,

My name is Nat Baldwin and I got your email from our mutual friend, Hollis Mickey. I imagine we have lots of other mutual friends, too, writers and musicians in the Providence area and beyond. I'm writing to you now because I have my first book coming out and I'm doing the thing that I guess authors are supposed to do and that is ask other authors they like for a blurb.

I thought of you because, honestly, I'm not sure I would be writing, or at least writing in the way that I write, had I not encountered Another Governess/The Least Blacksmith. It still blows me away, as does your newer and older work that I've read since (Dan, Man's Companions). I'm trying to ask people that I do not know personally (I admit I broke the rule already) to write blurbs in order to avoid the awkward friends doing favors for friends situation. So seeing as I don't know you, yet, and also have the highest respect for your creative powers, I thought you'd be a great candidate for the task.

The book is called The Red Barn and it's out this spring from Calamari Archive.

Here's a short piece that is very representative of the overall tone: http://thefanzine.com/the-fathers-face/

Of course, I totally understand if you are either not interested or just too busy and unable. I'd be totally honored if you even considered this request. Please let me know at your leisure.

Thanks,
Nat

The story you send as an example, "The Father's Face," appears in the online journal *Fanzine*, published by soliciting editor Danniel Schoonebeek, and is also included in *MCFX — An Anthology of the First 10 Years of the Mission Creek Festival*, published by Spork Press and coedited by festival programming directors Andre Perry, Joseph Tiefenthaler, and Christopher Wiersema.

Ruocco responds on December 18th, 2016, at 4:32 pm.

Hi Nat,

Congratulations on your book! I really love your music, and I'm excited to read your writing. Please send The Red Barn! What's the timeframe for the blurb? I think we do have a lot of mutual friends, probably about as many as it's possible for us to have without actually knowing each other. Maybe we will continue to accumulate mutual friends until it is a kind of Sophie Calle styled art project and we are each the other's missing piece from the social whole. Or maybe we will meet! In any event, or for now, I look forward to getting to know you through your work.

Very best,
Joanna

You receive the blurb on January 18th, 2017, at 10:03 pm.

Ruocco also writes romance novels under the pseudonyms Tori Jones, Joanna Lowell, and Alessandra Shahbaz.

MCFX also features work from Cornelius Eady, Brian Evenson, Tarfia Faizullah, Roxane Gay, Amelia Gray, Lindsay Hunter, Leslie Jamison, Mark Leidner, Jamaal May, Ander Monson, Kiki Pertrosino, and Jenny Zhang.

On February 11th, 2017, at an AWP off-site reading in Washington DC at Rhizome, you meet for the 1st time both Ruocco, who participates in the reading, and Joyelle McSweeney, who attends.

While much of his literary fiction could be described as psychological horror, Evenson also writes popular fiction categorized more clearly in the horror genre using the pen name B.K. Evenson.

You co-host the Rhizome event (with Claire Donato)—*Am I a Monster or Is This What It Means to Be a Person?*—the title taken from Clarice Lispector's final work, *The Hour of the Star*.

The epigraph for *Altmann's Tongue* comes from Julia Kristeva:

> *… more and more incisive, precise, eschewing seduction in favor of cruelty…*

The lineup features authors from Action Books, Calamari Archive, Per Second Press, and Tarpaulin Sky, including J'Lyn Chapman, Stanley Crawford, Johannes Göransson, Brandon

Hobson, Robert Lopez, Vi Khi Nao, Julie Reverb, Joanna Ruocco, and Abe Smith, among others.

Altmann's Tongue also features a blurb from Gilles Deleuze, appearing on the back cover of his FC2 collection, *The Wavering Knife*.

The audio version of *The Red Barn* is released on May 13th, 2022 on your label Tripticks Tapes, featuring 4 of the stories read alongside 2 tracks of double bass improvisations.

The opening section of the title track:

> *With my fist I scrape the taste out. Drop my pack to the dirt. The kids huddle close in the dark. We will soon get to work. But now no one can talk. I lock the latch. Take out the new tools. I tell the kids that today we will work all day. I point to the door bolted shut. They turn in unison, nod their heads yes. I point to windows, boarded up and black. I say how will we know when today's day is done? Their blank faces stare. I say when we are done with the work is how we will know. I say it may be a long day. Or maybe many days. But first thing's first. We need to clean the new tools thick with dust from the town. I say to the kids form a straight line. They hold their little hands out. They open their empty mouths. They take in their hands the tools I hand them. They lick the dust from the tools with the wet of their tongues. Then they pass the tools back to my hand. I examine their work. Most miss spots. Only one passes. The good kid again. So I set him aside. Hand him a new tool. I advise him to aim for the backs of their heads. I whisper in his ear so no one else can hear. I say just one strike, that much work lies ahead. But do not take it easy on them. When the good kid*

is done I lead him into the shed. I wipe him off. Adjust all his angles. Strip the clothes from his skin. He knows to keep quiet. I say you have done good. More words I whisper. He closes his eyes. The good kid listens.

You do not listen to the 1st bass improvisation while recording the 2nd, attempting to recreate it from memory while listening only to the recitation of the text, each track recorded in one take.

You start Tripticks Tapes in 2020, beginning with your solo release *AUTONOMIA III: Endnotes*, followed by Patrick Shiroishi's *Resting At the Heart of Green Shade*.

Endnotes is a journal/book series published by a discussion group "primarily oriented towards conceptualizing the conditions of possibility of a communist overcoming of the capitalist mode of production—and of the multiple structures of domination which pattern societies characterized by that mode of production—starting from present conditions," based in Germany, the UK and the US, originally forming in Brighton, UK in 2005.

In addition to *Tripticks*, Ann Quin publishes the novels *Berg, Three*, and *Passages*, while the posthumous collection, *The Unmapped Country: Stories and Fragments*, appears in 2018, edited by Jennifer Hodgson.

[Endnotes] was founded on a commitment to ruthlessly honest, open-ended internal debate, in which no topics would be off-limits, and in which the conversation itself was to be given priority over concerns about publishing, political position-taking or other matters in which the Ego—collective or individual—would necessarily take centre-stage.

AUTONOMIA II: Recombinations appears on Portland, ME-based label Traced Objects in 2020.

The Red Barn audio book shares a release show with Weston Olencki's *Old Time Music,* also released on Tripticks Tapes, at 10 Forward, in Greenfield, MA.

> *Ann Quin's Tripticks offers an episodic account of the narrator's flight across a surreal American landscape, pursued by his "No. 1 X-wife" and her new lover. This masterpiece of pre-punk aesthetics critiques the hypocrisy and consumerism of modern culture while spoofing the "typical" maladjusted family, which in this case includes a father who made his money in ballpoint pens and a mother whose life revolves around her overpampered, all-demanding poodle. Stylistically, this is Quin's most daring work, prefiguring the formal inventiveness of Kathy Acker.*

The description on the back of the Dalkey Archive edition of the book, above.

After reading the 1st few sections of "The Red Barn" you are joined by Jake Meginsky for a short duo improvisation, while a trio featuring Mary Staubitz, Arkm Foam, and Vic Rawlings also appears on the bill.

The show also marks the 1st installment of your short-lived series, Sibilants.

The 1st show you organize at the venue is the album release for *Tunnel To Light* by Travis Laplante and Jason Nazary, appearing on Tripticks in September 2021, the 9th release in the catalog.

Lispector's *The Passion According to G.H.* begins with an epigraph from art historian Bernard Berenson:

> *A complete life may be one ending in so full identification with the non-self that there is no self to die.*

Your 1st performance of the *AUTONOMIA: Body Without Organs* material takes place on August 26th, 2019 at Apohadion Theater in Portland, ME as part of id m theft able's Does series.

On February 28th, 2020, your solo tour in support of the above release begins in Baltimore, MD at The Red Room with Lexie Mountain, each performing solo sets before closing the night in collaboration.

Noy Holland's debut collection *The Spectacle of the Body* is published in 1994 by Knopf.

Each of the 3 *AUTONOMIA* releases are recorded on Peaks Island in Portland, ME by Peter McLaughlin, who you collaborate with on numerous projects, including the "Yankee Charms" east coast tours with the west coast-based Little Wings, the moniker of songwriter and visual artist Kyle Field.

The 1st line in your notebook filled with short phrases transcribed from Holland's workshop reads:

> *Creating more and more implications (not explications)…*

You see Stella Silbert and Neil 'Cloaca' Young perform at 10 Forward on August 23rd, 2021, possibly your 1st time at the venue, having moved to Western Mass from Portland, ME earlier in the month.

> *Maybe I should leave. Undecided I moved round the various houses, followed by the dogs. On my journey I took note that my car was no longer parked in the same place, but in another area, facing a main track. Rain was heavy. A few shadowy blanketed shapes passed, padding up and down ladders. A large group of men sat in a circle on the kiva roof, where a ladder leading into the kiva itself made two spires against the darkening sky. How unlike those iron stairs of the subway: the turnstile a symbol of authority, a meter of the capitalist system, a regulator of human movement, a metal-petalled flower of law and order. And like hell I was part of that system that turned men into well-fed and well-cared for pigs only interested in consumption and excretion.*

You return to Maine on September 1st, 2021 to prepare for the Little Wings "Yankee Charms II" tour, beginning on Peaks Island the next day.

An excerpt above the above fragment taken toward the end of *Tripticks*.

Grips, your duo with double bassist Amanda Irarrázabal, documents a live performance at IRL in Brooklyn on August 12th, 2021, the show presented by Jessica Hallock, aka NYC Noise, released on Tripticks Tapes exactly one year later on August 12th, 2022.

On August 13th, 2022, you perform in a trio with Silbert and Webb Crawford, whose *Joiners* is released on Tripticks just weeks later, at an event presented by NYC Noise at Ridgewood Presbyterian Church in Queens, NY.

"Saturating the senses" follows that 1st line, before a quote from Eileen Myles:

> *… it's not chaos, it's an organized dream…*

You perform with Silbert for the 1st time on December 2nd, 2021, at 10 Forward, the 1st night of a Bill Nace residency.

> *… vary where repetition happens… invention of structure through repetition … the endless malleability of the page…*

Playbackers' *Playbackers Record* appears on Tripticks in March 2023, the 33rd release in the catalog, the group featuring Foam, Silbert, and Young and recorded by Donny Shaw, who takes the place of Young in the current lineup.

On March 3rd, 2022, you perform in a trio with Chris Corsano and Jen Gelineau, night one of Corsano's residency at the venue.

> *… we are obdurately ourselves… the story is larger than you are… get out of the way of intent…*

During your 1st year living in Western Mass, the year prior to attending University, you also release 3 albums recorded before the move with Portland, ME-based collaborator E. Jason Gibbs—*Microstates, Phase Planes,* and *The Only Sound Is the Sound of the Sun Burning the Lake*.

Your 1st release with Silbert, *01.30.22*, recorded, mixed, and mastered by Olencki, is recorded at 10 Forward and titled after the recording date, appearing the following year on Notice Recordings.

The latter title referenced above the above fragment is taken from "The Spaces Between Teeth" in *The Red Barn*, which emerges through a prompt from Peter Markus to compose a story made of monosyllabic words, structured in 12 sections, each section containing 12 sentences, each sentence containing 12 words, to then use as a foundation to create a new work unbound by the initial constraints.

> *… polyphony within the form… the multi-voiceness of experience… inhabit the multiplicity…*

Brian Evenson writes the introduction to the Dalkey Archive edition of Ann Quin's 2nd novel, *Three*.

A trio with Paul Flaherty and Jake Meginsky on August 27th, 2022, at 10 Forward, is your last performance before your 1st semester at University.

Quin's fiction refuses the consolation of neat closure, says Evenson.

The show is recorded but, at the time of writing this text, not yet released.

> *…forestall the act of knowing…*

After teaching for 25 years at MFA for Poets & Writers, Noy Holland retires in 2022.

In the year prior to admittance, your 1st attempt applying to the Graduate Program in Experimental Music/Composition at University is unsuccessful.

After no response to your initial email about the tutorial, you follow up directly with Professor Martin on July 10th, 2023, who responds 27 minutes later, asking you to resend the email.

You cut and paste the email into your response, adding the following:

> *The "self-reflexive" stuff has become less annoying (I hope) and much less present as the work has evolved. I'd also add that I'd much prefer a one-on-one situation, as opposed to the seminar, both for the nature of the work and also to allow for more schedule flexibility (I'm commuting from Western Mass for the upcoming year). Otherwise, the rest of the above seems pretty accurate.*

Martin responds quickly and with much enthusiasm for the project, but alludes to a busy schedule and adds that tutorials are generally only offered within the department.

You follow up with Professor Vogel the next day.

Just prior to the initial email about the writing tutorial, you submit a research grant proposal in the form of a letter to the music department at University.

You present the proposal here in its entirety in earlier drafts of this chapter, previously titled "Labyrinth of Differentiations."

Professor Vogel responds, on July 24th, 2023, agreeing to the tutorial.

The proposal is clearly submitted before the shift to 2nd person, and before the self-reflexive editing fragments take on a dramatically reduced role, based on your description of the text.

You reference a quote from Alain Badiou, but do not include it in the proposal.

> *Infinite alterity is quite simply what there is. Any experience at all is the infinite deployment of infinite differences. Even the apparently reflexive experience of myself is by no means the intuition of a unity but a labyrinth of differentiations, and Rimbaud was certainly not wrong when he said: 'I am another.' There are as many differences, say, between a Chinese peasant and a young Norwegian professional as between myself and anybody at all, including myself.*

Before your 1st meeting, you are asked to fill out a questionnaire—"Intentions, Mysteries, Companions."

> *… what's most difficult has the greatest potential…*

The closing question reads:

> *Who are some of your companions? In other words, whose work do you imagine yours in conversation with?*

In a craft talk on audience and point of view, Noy offers a handout with some of her own notes to guide the discussion.

> *I begin, I think, not with knowing but with unrest, which is a form of a question, and the questions persist, and I end most anything I write not a whit wiser for it. I don't read*

or write fiction for answers, but for the feeling of being at
swim amid the muchness of what cannot be answered. So
much cannot be answered. Fiction is a way of remembering
this, even accepting this.

You underline short phrases in the above excerpt, including
the last sentence.

The only phrase underlined in your notebook:

> *… write the story that most spends you…*

Becoming Silent

The day after the Littoral event that you share with Brian Evenson and David Ohle, ISSUE Project Room presents an evening of collaborations between Bhob Rainey and Jason Lescalleet, nmperign and Sean Meehan, and Lescalleet and Graham Lambkin.

In the early 2000s, you frequently attend shows at the Zeitgeist Gallery in Cambridge, MA, seeing nmperign perform many times, a duo featuring Greg Kelley on trumpet and Bhob Rainey on soprano saxophone.

nmperign's style is often referred to as "lowercase" music, aligning with the "reductionist" scenes emerging at the time in Berlin, Vienna, and London, as well as the "ônkyo" scene in Tokyo.

> *The thing that does differentiate our kind of improvisation (if you will) from more traditional free improvisation is that*

there is often a sort of evolved consciousness of the fact that not everything has to be in every improvisation… One sometimes says, 'we're just going to stay in this field—that's exciting enough.'

In your 1st semester at University, in a required course called World Music Studies Proseminar, you write a research paper titled "Absence As Presence: Improvised Music In Tokyo and Berlin At the Turn of the Century."

Berlin-based percussionist Burkhard Beins, quoted in the fragment above the above fragment, features heavily in the paper in the sections on Berlin's *echtzeitmusik* scene.

You initially plan to incorporate nmperign and the Boston scene into the paper, even inquiring with Kelley about a potential interview, but instead decide to keep the focus on Tokyo and Berlin.

Echtzeitmusik translates loosely to "real-time music."

The "points of reference" section on the nmperign Wikipedia page states:

Despite the fact that the title of their first album was not a reference to John Cage (but simply the total time of the album divided by the number of tracks), nmperign has used a number of literary and other references in their titles, ranging from Marguerite Duras' The Malady of Death and Four Novels, Georges Bataille's Poems, Zen Master Eihei Dogen, a book of interviews with Jean-Luc Godard, Herman Melville's Pierre; Or, the Ambiguities, a box of Chinese tea, The Doors and micromosaic artist Henry Dalton.

You have read none of the above, but read Marguerite Duras' *The Ravishing of Lol Stein* while composing this text.

nmperign's first album *44'3"/5* is released on Twisted Village in 1998.

The name *nmperign* is derived from the Latin phrase "igNotuM PER IGNotius," meaning "the unknown through the more unknown," says Wikipedia.

Kelley and Rainey travel to Europe in 2000, recording a short session with Beins and trumpeter Axel Dörner, released as *Nmperign + Dörner, Beins* by Twisted Village in 2002.

The Japanese word "onkyô" is often translated by Western press as simply "sound," but a more accurate interpretation expresses the way sound interacts with space—*reverberation, echo.*

> *It could be said that the moment one recognizes a certain sound in terms of meaning, one stops hearing the sound as sound.*

Otomo Yoshihide, quoted above, and Sachiko M begin collaborating as a duo in 1995, performing more regularly after Otomo's influential group Ground Zero disbands in 1998, originally calling themselves A-102, or simply "duo," before using the name Filament exclusively after their 1st international tour to France and the US in May 1998.

Using an empty sampler to produce sine waves, Sachiko Matsubara performs as Sachiko M, releasing her debut solo album *Sine Wave Solo* in 1999 on Amoebic.

> *I simply wanted to listen to sounds more deeply… I think these*

*musicians' focuses are on hearing the sound, not physically
playing musical instruments.*

Sachiko M also collaborates with vocalist Ami Yoshida in
their duo Cosmos, their debut album *Tears* released in 2002
on US-based Erstwhile Records.

Erstwhile founder Jon Abbey starts the AMPLIFY festival
in 2002, the 1st held at Tonic in NYC, the 2nd only a few
months later in Tokyo (subtitled "Balance") featuring 12
sets across 3 nights—4 composed of all Japanese musicians,
4 all European, and 4 mixed—documented and released as
a 7CD+DVD box set.

Ami Yoshida releases *Spiritual Voice* in 1997 on 1040, and
Tiger Thrush in 2003 on Improvised Music From Japan, the
latter featuring 99 untitled tracks.

The festival is presented in Berlin in 2004, and again in
Tokyo in 2006 and 2008.

> *At the beginning I thought about "vocalizing" and the kinds
> of expression that were possible with it. Then I realized that
> I didn't want to "vocalize"—I wanted to "put out sound." I
> started thinking that electronic sound and more inorganic
> stuff were really interesting—so when I made the album,
> I wanted people to listen to it simply as sound, rather than
> think, "it's amazing that she can make these sounds with
> her voice."*

Yoshida is also known in Japan as a writer, poet, and comic
book critic, with one published novel, though the majority
of her writing has not yet been translated to English.

Improvised Music From Japan begins publishing an annual print magazine in 2002, releasing 6 issues, most with English translations, filled with interviews, reviews, concert notes and essays, as well as an accompanying compilation CD.

Yoshida's short story "Tiger Thrush" is featured in 2 parts in the 1st 2 publications of the magazine, translated by Cathy Fishman.

In 2009, Yoshida and Toshimaru Nakamura release *Soba to Bara* on Erstwhile Records, each recording their own solo tracks without listening to the other.

Nakamura's 1st solo album, *No-Input Mixing Board*, is released in 2000 on Zero Gravity.

No-Input Mixing Board 2 and *No-Input Mixing Board 3* follow soon after.

> *I find an equal relationship with no-input mixing board, which I didn't see with the guitar. When I played the guitar, "I" had to play the guitar. But with the mixing board, the machine would play me and the music would play the other two, and I would do something or maybe nothing. I would think some people would play the guitar and create their music with this kind of attitude, but for me, no-input mixing board gives me this equal relationship between the music, including the space, the instrument, and me.*

You are unaware of the "onkyô" scene when you first encounter nmperign.

The BSC, a Boston-based ensemble founded in 2000, features Kelley and Rainey alongside Mike Bullock (double bass),

James Coleman (theremin), Chris Cooper (prepared guitar), Vic Rawlings (cello, electronics), Howard Stelzer (tapes), and Liz Tonne (voice).

Their first album *Good* is released in 2003 and features Axel Dörner and Andrea Neumann, who were at the time of the recording about to join nmperign on a month-long tour of the US.

Neumann plays "inside piano," a modified piano of her own creation that removes the keys, hammers, pedals, and body, leaving just the soundboard and strings, using various everyday objects as preparations, amplifying the surface with contact mics and guitar pickups running to a mixer.

Beins, Dörner, and Neumann are all part of the group Phosphor, along with Robin Hayward (tuba), Annette Krebs (guitar, electronics), Michael Renkel (acoustic guitar), and Ignaz Schick (turntable, electronics), also forming in 2000.

You see all BSC members perform at the Zeitgeist Gallery in the early 2000s in smaller group configurations, but do not recall seeing the full ensemble.

The BSC Manual, edited by Rainey and released in 2011 on NO Books, features texts by Bullock, Rainey, Ben Hall, Damon Krukowski, and Aaron P. Tate, as well as a CD of a live performance by the group in collaboration with Pauline Oliveros.

Although they primarily engage with collective improvisation, the BSC are also known to perform the graphic scores of Oliveros, Cornelius Cardew, Karlheinz Stockhausen, and Christian Wolff.

Echtzeitmusik Berlin: Self-Defining a Scene, a collection featuring over 50 contributors edited by Burkhard Beins, Christian Kesten, Gisela Nauck, and Andrea Neumann, is published by Wolke Verlag in 2011, in German with English translations.

The complete list of citations in "Absence As Presence" includes work from Tom Arthurs, Burkhard Beins, Clive Bell, Matthew Blackwell, Marta Blažanović, Axel Dörner, Björn Gottstein, Robin Hayward, Christian Kesten, Toshimaru Nakamura, Gisela Nauck, Andrea Neumann, David Novak, Yoshio Otani, Lorraine Plourde, Sachiko M, Ignaz Schick, Shūhei Hosokawa, David Toop, Kazue Yokoi, Ami Yoshida, and Otomo Yoshihide. Improvised Music From Japan's magazine and *Echtzeitmusik Berlin* generate the majority of the material in the paper.

After the series of quotes from the 1998 Boston Globe article ("Coach Denies Player's Charge"), the final quote appearing at the end of this chapter, just before the closing 4 fragments, comes from Bhob Rainey's *BSC Manual* introduction.

In the fall of 2002, you share a bill with nmperign at the Flywheel in Easthampton, MA.

The same night, you think, that Jessica, or Jackson, delivers the news about the tubist, Eli Heilbrun.

The nmperign set at the Flywheel is in collaboration with Jason Lescalleet.

You perform in a quartet with Jack Wright on saxophone, Tom Djll on trumpet, and Eric Rosenthal on drums.

Two days prior to the performance, you record with Wright

and Djll, who are on tour together, along with drummer Mike Pride, at Pride's apartment in Brooklyn, NY.

Djll supposedly changes the spelling of his name, originally Dill, so that he can more easily google himself, according to Pride.

On Jack Wright's website, you finds a link to Djll's blog with a section documenting the 2002 tour.

From the entry labeled "September 4th, Easthampton, MA, The Flywheel":

> *Jack had invited the bassist from the Brooklyn session, who was young and didn't have a helluva lot of chops, saying, "He can't get in the way." But his sound, amplified, did get in the way. It filled up the whole floor, carpeting over many of Eric's punctuations. The set started off free-jazzy, which I wasn't in the mood for, either. And it was pretty loud, for the first twenty minutes. Eventually, some music got made, but there's no tape to prove it.*

You realize the date listed above is actually prior to Eli Heilbrun's death on October 2nd, 2002, so your memory seems to be conflating 2 separate but nearby events.

The nmperign show may have been with Sterno, a collaborative group with Brett Deschenes (trumpet), Mary Halvorson (guitar), and Dan St. Clair (piano), one of your few shows outside of University campus.

You reunite with Sterno on January 6th, 2024 at The Stone in NYC, the group's 1st performance in over 20 years, the closing night of Halvorson's residency at the venue.

The 1st time you perform with Jessica Pavone is at The Kitchen in NYC on July 11th, 2001, with The String Army, an ensemble she co-founds with bassist Seth Dellinger.

Solo double bass and voice performances by Dellinger at the time are an influence on your dense, stamina-driven pieces on *Solo Contrabass*, while nmperign, as well as the Vienna-based group Polwechsel, can be traced to the more sparse, event-based works.

The latter material in reference above—"Mask," "FM," "And Two Wires"—are all composed using graphic scores with symbols or abbreviated codes that determine the structure and content.

"FM" uses 3 vertical columns to separate actions for left hand, right hand, and bow, at times employing multiple overlapping gestures, while always maintaining extremely low dynamics.

Polwechsel's self-titled debut features Werner Dafeldecker (double bass, guitar), Michael Moser (cello), Radu Malfatti (trombone), and Burkhard Stangl (guitar), while their 2nd and 3rd releases replace Malfatti with John Butcher (saxophones) and add electronics to Dafeldecker's credits.

Active since 1993, the group currently features Dafeldecker and Moser alongside percussionists Burkhard Beins and Martin Brandlmayr.

polwechsel were among the first groups of this multifaceted music scene to establish aesthetic strategies and performance practices that were soon recognised as a radical form of ›reductionism‹: a paring down of the habitual musical linguisticality in favour of a microscopic exploration of singular musical events; a deceleration and deautomation of musical processes in favour of immersive listening; an eschewing of the dramaturgy of musical forms in favour of focussing attention on the fleeting presence and physical materiality of sound; an awareness of the flip-side of sound, of background noises, silence, disruptions in sound production and musical articulation. the music seemed to rebel against the information we are being flooded with through the current modes of social communication just as it invited the listener to discover a whole world in the neglected, imperfect, confusing detail — an ordinary world perhaps or even a counterworld, but certainly not a refuge. perhaps the minimal, measured gesture that produced this music also took a sceptical look at the creative enthusiasm and innovative drive which had come to dominate the post-fordist working practices. the reductionism of the time was a school of perception that linked the protagonists of vienna's experimental music scene to berlin echtzeitmusik, japanese onkyo and new london silence. it still serves as a common horizon of that generation of musicians, but belongs to the past. as michael moser said about the work at that time, »to reduce further would mean to stop playing«, that is, to become silent.

You ignore potential edits in the above review excerpt by Matthias Haenisch and present it as it appears on the Polwechsel website.

In the spring of 2002, as many friends at University graduate and make their next move, you begin to feel isolated and creatively stuck, while some deeply buried personal issues from the past begin to rise to the emotional surface, ultimately leading to a hiatus from music altogether before *Solo Contrabass* is even released.

A primary motivation to move near University after receiving the initial rejection from admissions revolves around the intention to reapply at the end of the academic year, in hopes that auditing Professor Braxton's classes and immersing yourself in the community will lead to an acceptance.

> *The boy's mother said that at one point she noticed that her son, typically even-keeled, became morose and suffered from insomnia.*

After a long meeting in his office, Braxton writes you a glowing recommendation, the original and its copy still sitting in a manila folder envelope in your desk, over 20 years later, your name misspelled as "Nate" at the top.

> *"This is really about standing up," said attorney Jim Noucas, who is representing the family. "It's a matter of responsibility."*

Upon hearing the news that you did not in fact reapply, Braxton walks quickly away in silence and you have not spoken since.

> *"He used our son's love for basketball," said the boy's father. "He had dinner with us, at our home. He worked to gain our trust."*

At the tournament in Providence, RI, when you see Chris Herren, the "basketball junkie," play for the 1st time, another onlooker, a stout, rotund man with glasses, stands nearby, initiating a conversation with you, 14 at the time.

*The alleged inappropriate contact was the culmination of a
relationship that even [the coach's] supporters say was unique,
with the former player staying at [the coach's] home on some
weekends to review game tapes.*

After abandoning plans to reapply to University, you move
home.

*Several sources familiar with the Greater Boston program,
and the boy's parents, say that he arrived on the team with
decent playing ability, but thrived under [the coach's] coaching, and headed into his senior year with hopes of winning
a college scholarship.*

During the creative pause, burdened by a blurred sense of
self, you contact the coaching staff at nearby State College.

*The teenager who alleged the sexual advances has requested
anonymity.*

You enroll and commit to the team's summer conditioning
program, arriving for the fall 2003 semester in peak physical
form.

On the official release day for *Solo Contrabass,* you are running hill sprints in a cemetery and haven't touched your
bass in months.

Just weeks into the semester, you withdraw from classes
without telling anyone, and again, return home.

*The forms surrounding significant moments in the past can
rarely be relied upon to conjure up significant moments in
the present.*

While tracking down the Boston Globe article during the composition of this text, you find [the coach's] obituary.

The date marked beneath the name, next to a photograph—
September 1st, 2021.

There are only a few comments on the "tribute wall."

The cause of death is not disclosed.

SIDE B

Species of Spaces
and Other Pieces

In the 1st-year Composition Seminar at University, you compose one composition.

The composition is to be written for the visiting ensemble, with permission to write oneself into the piece if one desires, which you do.

There will be one 30-minute meeting on Zoom, and one 30-minute rehearsal the day before the performance.

The visiting ensemble is called String Noise, a duo of violin virtuosos composed of Conrad Harris and Pauline Kim Harris.

Your piece is composed through a series of text instructions, marking each section by time.

While the options within in each section of the piece are limited, the performers are given choices as to how to navigate the material.

You handwrite the score, scan copies, and send to String Noise, approximated as follows:

[SIBILANTS] <u>*Nat Baldwin*</u> *+* <u>*String Noise*</u>   *[Fall 2022]*

> *(Operate independently unless alignment is*
> *indicated. Soft dynamics throughout)*

~<u>*TIME*</u> *-* <u>*SECTION*</u> *-* <u>*INSTRUCTIONS*</u>

> *single bow strokes, sounding harmonics:*

Harmonic Double Stops - bass [A/B] - violin left [E/F#] - violin right [B/C#]
> *— choice of range, but keep pitches constant throughout section*
> *— begin on single lower harmonic, add 2nd before bow runs out*
> *— silence between each gesture*
> *— vary durations of gesture/silence*

1'30"(Vs) RH Gestures
2' (B)   CR = bow pressure / angled motion to produce slow "crackle" sound
SW = quick downward stroke near frog for sharp "swipe" sound
BB = slow bow at bridge, can sound harmonic or not
SP = spiccato - can vary btw 1 string / X-strings (any
direction) / instr. body
> *— cycle through gestures in any order at own pace*
> *— vary silences btw gestures*
> *— LH dampen strings throughout, sometimes*
> *scratching lightly w/ fingernails*

4' Short Double Stops - alternate btw P5 / m2 - players choice, keep
*   same throughout*
*   — continue to interject above gestures between each double stop*
*   — vary length of double stops as section progresses*

5'30" Drop gestures / Continue double stops

6' (B) Spiccato Repeats
6'30"(Vs) — X-strings from low to high, silence btw each gesture
*   — LH damp*
*   — violins begin section independently from bass, attempt*
*   to align before the end*

7'   *[THE END]*

. *enthusiastic audience clapping sounds* .

Encyclopedia Britannica defines "sibilant" as "a fricative con-
sonant sound, in which the tip, or blade, of the tongue is
brought near the roof of the mouth and air is pushed past
the tongue to make a hissing sound."

You have not yet received the Zoom H4n Pro Handy Recorder
and do not document the performance, which takes place on
December 10th, 2022.

Program notes:

A collection of small sounds and static gestures overlapping
and interacting with space.

***

On February 23rd, 2023, you receive a Zoom H4n Pro Handy Recorder, a gift from Stella Silbert, along with *Word Events: Perspectives On Verbal Notation.*

When you return to University after the weekend at home, you record sound sources for a fixed media 8-channel piece for the Sound Systems and Chamber Electronics class mid-term project to be performed the following week in a large room with a large sound system while live-mixing the tracks on a 32-channel mixer.

There are 4 tracks of fixed sound sources, each performed on double bass and recorded in one take with the Zoom H4n Pro Handy Recorder, your 1st time using the device, documented in further detail in the recording documentation section of the text.

1 bows / trem
2 bows / trem
3 low d / spic
4 low d / spic

1 bows
2 trem
3 low d
4 spic

1 x
2 x
3 low d
4 x

1 wires
2 wires
3 low d - x - harm
4 harm

1 x
2 x
3 harm
4 harm

The above outline is the only version of something resembling a score for the piece, typed into the Notes app on your phone in the middle of the night on February 26th, 2023.

Moved from its original position in the "Field Recordings, Etc" document, the outline/score is the 1st entry in a new document called "Scores, Program Notes."

The numbers refer to each recording of fixed material, the actions of which are outlined in more detail in the "Field Recordings, Etc" chapter that documents each recording.

The actions corresponding to each number are then assigned 8 channels of the mixer.

Four tracks using 8 channels each equals 32 channels.

In addition to the fixed material, the composition takes shape through live diffusion—mixing the tracks across the 8 speakers in real time during the performance.

The speakers are placed in stereo pairs in the back of the stage area at the ceiling, front of the stage area at the ceiling, front of the stage area on the floor, and behind the audience seating at the ceiling.

After rehearsing the piece in the performance space, you write a basic outline to structure the mixing in your Notes app to refer to during the performance.

You do not recall referring to the outline much, if at all, instead relying on memory through preparation, as well as instinct and improvisation in response to the sounds in the space in real time.

The piece is arbitrarily and decisively titled *What Is To Be Done*.

For the program notes, you cut and paste text from the original "Field Recordings, Etc" document and add sentences to the beginning and end:

> *The sound sources consist of 4 unedited tracks of double bass. The 4 tracks are broken into pairs. On 2 tracks, the bass is played flat on its back. Sounds used: 2-bow tremolo above and below bridge with endpin preparation between finger-board and strings to dampen open strings, 2-bow tip perc with endpin and left foot damp, 2 wires between endpin and saddle right hand bow with left hand plucks below bridge. On the other 2 tracks, the bass is played upright in the conventional stance. Sounds used: detuned low D interruptions, improvisation centered around spiccato and textural harmonics, slow bow crackles, detuned low D drone, clean harmonics with melodic character. The sections are marked by time with staggered transitions.*

You notice 2 appearances of the word "the" in the original document after including the above text in the program notes.

You keep the above as is, while editing the original document.

After receiving *Sleepingfish* edits, documented in the next chapter, you change the numbers to #s above (and through-out the rest of the text).

You forget to bring Zoom H4n Pro Handy Recorder to the performance and there is no audio documentation of the piece.

***

In the 2nd semester of the 1st year at University, you join the Toneburst Laptop and Electronic Arts Ensemble, led by Professor Paula Matthusen.

You write a piece for the ensemble with the patch used to soundcheck at the beginning of each rehearsal.

The patch consists of silence, triangle wave, and pink noise.

There's an overall volume control, as well as a frequency range that can be activated within the triangle wave setting.

The score reads as a set of instructions, with time and dynamic markings, as follows:

[section 1 - STATIC EVENTS] ~ 0'00"~2'30" /// medium loud - medium quiet

0'00" play triangle wave between frequency range 11–10001 (5~10 seconds to start) /// medium loud

make one of 3 choices: stop playing triangle wave (silence); play new triangle wave (emphasize frequency contrast); play pink noise (5~10 seconds to start)

continue to repeat above 2 directions (beginning with new triangle wave, moving onto new choices), increasing rate of activity as section progresses

~2'00"~2'30" choose frequency to repeat throughout next section between range of 2 options: LOW = < 50; HIGH = > 9000 /// medium quiet

[section 2 - DRONE CUTS] ~ 2'30"~5'00" /// medium quiet/medium

~2'30" continue triangle wave that ends previous section

~2'45" introduce brief pink noise interruptions before quickly returning to your wave (use space between each interruption, centering on the wave)

~3'00" add silence as interruption and cycle through silence / triangle wave / pink noise in any order with varied durations

~3'30" experiment with pulse and rhythm as you shift between events, moving in and out of repetitions and looped

patterns

after establishing some patterns, introduce more space and loosen the patterns

~4'30"~4'50" silence with wave interruptions (no pink noise)

4'50"-5'00" silence

[section 3 - OSCILLATION SWELLS] *~ 5'00"~8'00"*
/// loud - medium - medium quiet

5'00" pink noise /// loud

~5'30"~5'45" if previous choice was low frequency wave, switch to high (btw 7000-7500), stagger entrances /// medium

~5'45"~6'00" if previous choice was high frequency wave, switch to low (btw 25-50), stagger entrances /// medium

after shifting to wave, choose between 2 options: oscillate frequency, within assigned range, at various speeds; or, dynamic swells at your own pace

~7'00" stop oscillating/swelling, settle into wave /// medium quiet

listen for cue - pink noise - to cut

to silence

///

The final concert takes place on May 10th, 2023 at WMH at University.

Your piece opens the show.

Program notes:

> */// C U T S /// explores a range of material available in the patch used to balance the collective amplitude of the ensemble at the beginning of each rehearsal.*

Ensemble members are scattered throughout the hall, and you occupy a far back corner up the steps in the audience.

You bring the Zoom H4n Pro Handy Recorder and are very pleased with the performance of the piece, but due to your position in the space, the recording comes out a bit quiet and unbalanced.

***

The final project in Sound Systems and Chamber Electronics must be executed using a program called SuperCollider.

At the end of the semester, after the performance of the projects, Professor Kuivila asks for a "final project report" using the following prompt:

> *You can think of this as a detailed expansion of your program note for your piece. It should describe the overall creative process, the hurdles you needed to overcome, and a comparison of your initial intentions for the project with how the project actually turned out.*

You submit the project report on May 16th, 2023, outlining 3 ideas that trace the development of the piece, which you have titled *Species of Spaces*.

> ***Idea #1:*** *Use March 4th, March 5th, March 6th, and March 7th recordings of coffee making at Alsop House, occupying their own speaker pairs to accommodate the stereo mix and spread across the 8 speakers in WMH. Each recording runs exactly 15 minutes, attempting to perform the actions in the exact order of the previous recordings by memory. Materials used: Hario Ceramic Coffee Mill, Hario Coffee Dripper, Hario V60 Paper Filter, Bonavita Gooseneck Kettle, 1992 Dream Team mug, Share Coffee Roasters coffee, water from sink on 2nd-floor bathroom. Original idea for repeated recordings of same actions emerge from a coincidence between a field recording made one day before class and the contents of a class discussion, both occurring on February 28th. The field recording consists of a long walk (a short walk that took a long time), going from Fairview Ave. to Alsop House on the morning after a snowstorm. Encounters on Foss Hill include the sounds of skiers, snowboarders, sledders, snowball throwers, and a direct interaction with a classmate just returning from the hospital to drop off a friend with a broken collarbone (before then continuing to ski off the homemade jump where the injury occurred). The sounds of social activity decrescendos with distance, while the sonic environment shifts drastically upon entering Alsop House. The daily ritual of making coffee closes the nearly 45-minute piece, highlighting the intimacy of routine and isolated actions in contrast to the lively dynamics and chaos on the hill. The most compelling sonic component of the coffee-making procedure occurs just as the water hits the ground beans for the first time, activating the bloom, slowly carving*

out the cone to direct the drips to the cup, the small crackles and pops amplified by close and careful placement of the microphone. In class later that day, we are shown a video of a John Cage piece, the name of which I can't remember, and the score of which asks the performer to perform an everyday task of their choice, or something of that nature, performed by a professor beginning class by making coffee for his students. I record the 4 coffee tracks after the experience, intrigued by the connection, unsure how I will use them but thinking their similarities and slight differences could provide interesting material in combination with each other. With the final project approaching, I think it could be a good opportunity to put the idea into action. However, when the professor responds in a meeting about the project that it sounds "cute" it's immediately clear I need to go a different direction. The professor also mentions he thought I might incorporate the mixer feedback I'd been exploring the previous semester, pushing me to rethink my approach, grateful for the encouragement and an excuse to dive back into the mixer.

Idea #2: Use 2 tracks of no-input mixer feedback improvisations to provide the foundation for an 8-channel piece, while incorporating previously made field recordings emphasizing the dynamic range of material produced throughout the semester, both in terms of sonic activity/approach as well as location/environment. After exploring various combinations of material to combine with the feedback tracks, 4 are chosen—March 17th, Millers Falls, MA: packing tape orders (materials used: scissors, scotch tape, bubble wrap, cassettes, padded envelopes, table); March 20th, Kittery Point, ME: fire on rocks near ocean; April 2nd, Middletown, CT: Twelfth Night rehearsal from open 3rd-floor window outside Alsop House (with headphone feedback and detached bow hair contact); April 16th, Middletown, CT: reading Experimental Music Since 1970 by Jennie Gottschalk before bed with fan on. The idea is that each recording enters one by one. Once all 8 channels are occupied, new material displaces the old. The structure looks something like this: no-input 1, no-input 2, tape, 12th night, fire (no-input 1 out), fan (no-input 2 out), fire (12th night out), fire (tape out), fire (fan out). By the end, all 8 channels are taken up by the fire field recording, displaced by staggered entrances, a quiet contrast to the harsh opening of feedback. Ultimately, this approach seemed too complicated within the context of the class and the timing of the final project. Additionally, many of the field recordings made thus far, including those used in this project draft, feel particularly personal in a way that presents challenges in the context of collage. The thinking may evolve, but it's difficult to detach the material from its original intent as 1st-person narratives occupying their own, intimate space.

Idea #3: *Eliminate the field recording ideas outlined above and focus on the no-input material. The 2 feedback tracks offer plenty to work with on their own, and a multichannel presentation only extends the possibilities. I assign each track 2 speaker pairs each: track 1 occupies speakers 1/2 and 5/6; track 2 occupies 3/4 and 7/8. I explore spatiality through sharp cuts and hard entrances, as opposed to slow fades and soft decay. Even in moments of inactivity, the slight static of the speaker pairs coming in and out provides sonic material that shapes the performance. The cutting, displacing, and relocating of the sounds in real time becomes a compositional component alongside the fixed material. Improvising the multichannel mix allows for new structures to emerge specific* *to each performance, influenced by interaction with unique sound systems and the architecture of their environment. The no-input tracks are not only the first recorded documents of my collaboration with the instrument, but they are also the first time I've felt truly comfortable on it, open to unpredictability and prepared to react.*

After you explain the basic idea articulated above, Professor Kuivila writes the following code:

```
(
~fpMaker = { | chan = 0, buf = 5, panL= -0.68, panR=0.68, rate = 1, db = 0 |
    { var audio;
            var pl = ("pan" ++ chan ++ "L").asSymbol;
            var pr = ("pan" ++ chan ++ "R").asSymbol;
            var r = ("rate" ++ chan).asSymbol;
            var d = ("db" ++ chan).asSymbol;
            Spec.add(pl, \bipolar);
            Spec.add(pr, \bipolar);
            Spec.add(r, [0.25, 4, 'exponential']);
            Spec.add(d, [-20, 20]);
            pl = pl.kr(panL);
            pr = pr.kr(panR);
            r = r.kr(rate);
            d = d.kr(0);
        audio = PlayBuf.ar(2, bufnum: buf, rate: r, loop: 0);
        audio = audio * d.dbamp;
//PanAz.ar(8, audio[0], pl) + PanAz.ar(8, audio[1], pr);
        Pan2.ar( audio[0], pl) + Pan2.ar(audio[1], pr);

    }
};
s.options.numOutputBusChannels = 10;
s.quit;
s.waitForBoot {
        // guarantee the server is running
```

```
~files = "audio/*".resolveRelative.pathMatch;
// find files in the folder "audio", which
~buffers = ~files.collect{ | f | Buffer.read(s, f) };
// load those sounds into buffers on the server


~np1 = NodeProxy.audio(s, 2);
~np2 = NodeProxy.audio(s, 2);


~np1.gui(5, Rect(873.0,600.0, 394.0, 150.0));
~np2.gui(5, Rect(873.0, 420.0, 394.0, 150.0));


s.sync;
~np1[1] = ~fpMaker.(1, ~buffers[0].bufnum);
~np2[1] = ~fpMaker.(2, ~buffers[1].bufnum);


        ~sp1 = NodeProxy.audio(s,2);
        ~sp2 = NodeProxy.audio(s,2);
        ~sp3 = NodeProxy.audio(s,2);
        ~sp4 = NodeProxy.audio(s,2);
        ~sp1[0] = { ~np1.ar };
        ~sp2[0] = { ~np1.ar };
        ~sp3[0] = { ~np2.ar };
        ~sp4[0] = { ~np2.ar };
        ~sp1g = ~sp1.gui(0, Rect(873.0, 350.0, 394.0, 30.0));
        ~sp1g = ~sp2.gui(0, Rect(873.0, 270.0, 394.0, 30.0));
        ~sp1g = ~sp3.gui(0, Rect(873.0, 190, 394.0, 30.0));
        ~sp1g = ~sp4.gui(0, Rect(873.0, 110, 394.0, 30.0));
        ~sp1.playN([0,1]); // channels 12
        ~sp2.playN([0,1] + 4).stop; // 56
        ~sp3.playN([0,1] + 2).stop; // 34
        ~sp4.playN([0,1] + 6).stop; // 78

};


~spg1


)
```

The John Cage piece you forget the name of is *0'00"*, the original score reads:

> *In a situation provided with maximum amplification (no feedback), perform a disciplined action.*

Program notes:

> *The sound sources consist of 2 feedback improvisations using no-input mixer, a Mackie 1202VLZ4 12-channel, recorded on May 1st and May 2nd in RHH105 with a Zoom H4n Pro Handy Recorder placed on a chair placed on a table. Both original tracks run 43'43" and have been chopped into a more appropriate length to fit the context of this concert, then routed to their own 2 pairs of speakers across the 8-channel system. A defining feature of the multichannel realization is to implement sharp cuts and entries that displace, erase, and relocate the fixed material in real time, using spatiality as a productive source of content and form that echoes the unpredictability of the instrument.*

In addition to the final project performance, you also perform a 4-channel version of the piece to begin a solo set at the 20 Years of Shinkoyo festival at Roulette, organized Matt Mehlan, on September 6th, 2023, just hours after receiving the news of Charles Gayle's death.

Second Person

You send a draft of the 1st and 2nd chapters, unnamed at the time and referred to as "sections," along with drafts of 2 of the compositions, *Sibilants* and */// C U T S ///*, to Cal A. Mari (in attendance at above-mentioned Roulette performance), upon an invitation to submit to the *Sleepingfish* 20-year-anniversary issue, co-edited by Garielle Lutz.

You also send, at the same time, the 1st chapter and the 1st composition mentioned above to Micah Silver.

The act of sending, along with the realization of readers engaging, especially those particular readers above, motivates significant edits that shift the structure and tone of the text.

The drafts are sent on July 17th, 2023.

Ten days later, you make clear to the editors that the work

should not be considered a submission.

Cal initially responds the day after the draft is sent, indicating some parts he likes and asking if you mind if the material is cut up and remixed.

> *hey just wanted to update that the excerpts i sent are seeing some major revisions. cutting lotsa stuff and trying 2nd person. the baumer/red barn stuff is gonna shift into a later section, most of that 2nd section is probably out. feels like it's in too early of a stage for anyone to try to take the time to chop it up and remix. i mostly just wanted to send to show what i've been up to, and even just knowing some discerning eyes were on it made me rethink some things, as it goes. thanks a bunch for checking it out.*

The primary change is a shift in narrator point of view from 3rd to 2nd person—"Student" becomes "you."

> *Yah, I can hold off on the remix. Looking forward to the edits, it was off to a good start.*

"Student" is a reference to the protagonists in David Markson's *Notecard Quartet: Reader's Block* ("Reader"), *This Is Not a Novel* ("Writer"), *Vanishing Point* ("Author"), *The Last Novel* ("Novelist").

The only books you recall reading that exclusively use 2nd person are *A Jello Horse* by Matthew Simmons, *Ablutions* by Patrick deWitt, and *Suicide* by Edouard Levé.

You read Gabi Losoncy's *Second Person* over summer break, published in 2017 by Amphetamine Sulphate.

If there were an epigraph at the beginning of this text, it might be from *Second Person*:

> *The more of you there are, the better off we are.*

The other significant change from the initial drafts is the removal of much of the self-reflexive material that refers to edits in the text as they are made.

The 1st appearance of such material occurs early in the draft of the 1st chapter:

> *Student edits out the word "the" from the above fragment 21 times.*

> *Also removed, just once each, are the words "his," "an," and "is."*

> *Student finds and cuts another "the" upon rereading, bringing the total to 22.*

> *Student cuts another "his," making that 2.*

> *In the fragment referenced in the above 4 fragments, Student changes the word "activity" to the word "action" 5 times.*

> *The above 5 fragments were written before the commitment to make all fragments in the primary section of the text a single sentence, before the omission of the word "the" is applied exclusively to the recording documentation section of the text, and before future editing sessions reverse much of the activity being referenced.*

Other content removed includes references to Ishmael Reed's daughter Timothy, Anna Kavan's father's suicide, Virginia Woolf's suicide, Ray Raposa's last album, and Peter Kowald's heart attack in William Parker and Patricia Nicholson's apartment after a performance you nearly attend.

The Charles Gayle material is a late addition to the 1st chapter.

Instead of ending with the Markson quotes, the 1st chapter draft ends:

> *Student replaces "is starting to fear" with "fears" above the fragment above the above fragment.*

> *The fragment referenced in the above fragment shifts when the fragment currently in that position takes its place.*

> *Student cuts the fragment referenced in the above 2 fragments.*

The only fragments from that version of the 2nd section that still exist in the current text are the Mark Baumer and *The Red Barn* release show material, reestablishing their positions in the chapter now titled "Slides of Color."

The only Baumer material that gets cut is the bio for Boots Walking In America included in a *Sleepingfish* issue (from a story that is reprinted in the 20th-anniversary issue), which initially appears after the section moves to "Slides of Color."

> *Boots Walking in America was born in America. He got his first library card before his left pupil fully opened. He*

was four. His mother had a bad grease rash on her face, but
he still loved her. When Boots Walking in America finally
became an adult he got a job at the local university gas
station. Later, he was promoted to emptying the van. He
has never left the continent.

The 2nd section quickly incorporates the most extensive use
of the self-reflexive edits, the indulgence perhaps marking
the beginning of the end of their primary role.

You then reference the origins and characteristics of horse
hair on bass bows, *The Red Barn* and "Let Me See the
Colts," Nietzsche's demise after witnessing the beating of
a horse, *The Turin Horse* by Béla Tarr, and your mom's job
as a horse-carriage driver.

The horse carriage becomes a way to talk about a man your
mom meets while working that becomes a very close family
friend, coming to all of your basketball games—including
the one that put you in the hospital with a serious concussion,
which you discuss in more detail in the cut material—your
biggest fan, who tragically ended his life, shooting himself
in the head when you were 15.

After introducing the Mark Baumer and *The Red Barn*
material, you end the draft of the 2nd section with the 1st
reference to the "(Cuts from) Antithesis" document and a
story of a brief interaction with a man outside your place of
employment at the time, just prior to attending University.

> *Student cuts over a page of fragments, beginning with one*
> *previously occupying this position, and places them in a new*
> *document titled "(Cuts from) Antithesis."*

While standing in front of the record shop on a slow day, Student is approached by a large man, about 6'6" or 6'7", with the same name as the name of the record shop, looking to be around the same age as Student, wearing a Knicks hat, which Student compliments.

He's been living on the street since walking from another town a bit west.

A fight with his girlfriend, he says.

Asks Student for some money, apologizing repeatedly.

Student gives the man some money.

The man thanks Student, repeatedly, they pound fists, the man goes on his way.

According to Google Maps, the town the man walked from is 41.3 miles away.

A few days later in the shop, a regular customer mentions to Student that a shooting happened the night before just a block away.

Unsure of the details, other than the victim's last known residence—the same town the man with the same name as the record shop claimed to have walked from.

He scored his 1000th point on January 26th, 2000, finishing his high school career with 1178 points, says the obituary.

A single gunshot wound to the head, according to reports.

He was always happiest when on the basketball court, the obituary says.

Student reaches the 1000-point milestone in the final game of the season, the final game of Student's career, finishing with 1020 in total, which must have been sometime in February 1999, a few months before leaving for Conservatory.

The above fragments below the fragment referencing "(Cuts from) Antithesis" were cut and (re)pasted from the beginning of the document "(Cuts from) Antithesis," with some additional cuts and edits.

It's difficult to trace the trajectory of the motion, as the "(Cuts from) Antithesis" document has become increasingly disorganized, but it seems the initial ideas for "Potential Literature" are incorporated into the 2nd section, or into material emerging from that section, before it becomes its own chapter.

You find a block of text prefaced with the heading *[at the end of the OULIPO section]* referencing the man referenced above, indicating it is either an extension of the 2nd section draft composed after it was sent to *Sleepingfish*, or part of an additional section meant to follow it that has also been cut.

The day referenced in the above fragment is March 5th.

Student cuts the fragments introducing the man referenced in the next fragment when Student makes the new document "(Cuts from) Antithesis."

The man who got shot in the head a few days after interacting with Student outside the record shop, who also had the same first name as the record shop, was born on March 5th, 1982.

Student shifts the fragment initially in this position above the above fragment, and replaces "above" with "next" between "the" and "fragment."

After editing and resending a submission for the *Sleeping-fish* 20th-anniversary issue, you cut the next 6 pages of this chapter following this fragment, consisting of references to chapters that no longer exist.

***

The above fragment marks the end of this chapter as it is presented in the *Sleepingfish* 20th-anniversary publication.

You think about adding "at the request of the editors" following the comma after "fragment" and before "consisting" in the fragment referenced in the above fragment, but decide to keep it as is in order to maintain the accuracy of the above fragment.

When you receive edits from Garielle Lutz, author of Calamari titles *Stories In the Worst Way*, *Divorcer*, and *The Gotham Grammarian*, among other works, she makes clear her confusion regarding your use of the word "fragment" to refer to isolated, single sentences.

Lutz's I Looked Alive is the only book you remember starting again immediately after finishing, reading a 2nd time in its entirety.

Your brother, Niles Baldwin, has 5 pieces of flash fiction

appearing in the *Sleepingfish* anniversary issue, his 1st print publication.

"The Last Page of Books" is the last page of the book.

> *He tried his tongue to the hand for the parts that wouldn't wash away.*

The issue also features work by Steven Alvarez, Rosaire Appel, Ali Aktan Aşkın, Maeve Barry, Chiara Barzini, Mark Baumer, Emilio Carrero, Kim Chinquee, David-Baptiste Chirot, Bobby Crace, Anna DeForest, Federico Federici, Noah Eli Gordon, Mariangela Guatteri, John Haskell, Chelsea Hogue, Tim Horvath, Zebulon House (or Horse), Meiko Ko, Kelly Krumrie, Mary Kuryla, Babak Lakghomi, Eugene Lim, Carlos M. Luis, John Madera, Peter Markus, Sawako Nakayasu, Elle Nash, David Nutt, Kim Parko, Nick Francis Potter, Rachterscale (aka Rachita Ramya), Carla Rak, Michael Salu, Sofia Samatar, Jonathan Sargent, Nina Shope, Jada Smiley, Elijah Sparkman, Justin Torres, Tor Ulven (tranlsated by Jordan Barger), Michel Vachey (translated by S. C. Delaney and Agnès Potier), Angela Woodward, and Yuxin Zhao.

One chapter from an earlier portion of the text that no longer exists, containing material removed before the final *Sleepingfish* submission, is "Crippled Symmetry," which begins and ends with references to Harry Crews.

> *"Knockout," from your 2014 release In the Hollows, draws inspiration from Harry Crews' novel The Knockout Artist, while "Cosmos Pose" is based on Crews' Body.*

You also thread some Crews biographical content into the closing section of "Slides of Color" before cutting, while the majority of "Crippled Symmetry" focuses on songwriting and lyrical references, alongside related material.

> *"Black Square" refers to Charlie Looker's "Back To the Black Square" composed for his group Lavender, the lineup at the time a quintet with Brett Deschenes, Mike Pride, and Karen Waltuch.*

In the year after leaving School of Music, in addition to Lavender, Middletown Creative Orchestra, Sterno, The String Army, and Braxton's orchestra at University, you also perform in collaborative duos with both Jeremy "Phloyd" Starpoli and Dan St. Clair, as well as an electroacoustic ensemble organized by Jesse Kudler called Phil Collins.

> *Like "Black Square," the songs "Dome Branches," "De-Attached," and "The Felled Trees" all appear on Most Valuable Player, while their titles reference compositions by Dan St. Clair originally written for Sterno.*

The one group you maintain during your 2nd and final year at School of Music, as you begin to shift energy toward activity at University, is Empty All, stylized as 01, a trio with Emre Ersenkal and Dan Voss.

> *The Most Valuable Player album cover is a photograph of your trophy for the N.E.P.S.A.C. Class C Tournament Most Valuable Player award from 1998, received after your high school basketball team wins the New England championship in your division.*

"Mask I Wear," the penultimate track on *Most Valuable Player*, consists nearly entirely of references to *Solo Contrabass*, the lyrics of which you include in their entirety in "Crippled Symmetry."

> *Brett Deschenes, Will Glass, Jeremy Lightcastle, and Alex Mead join you on a month-long tour for the release of Most Valuable Player in the winter of 2008.*

The above group also appears on "Lifted" from the follow-up release, *People Changes*.

The closing track on *Most Valuable Player*, "Look She Said," takes its title from a Christian Wolff piece for solo double bass, while the lyrics name titles of works by Morton Feldman:

> *False Relationships and the Extended Ending, Why Patterns?, Crippled Symmetry.*

In addition to "Mask I Wear," the chapter also includes the lyrics to "Weights," the 2nd track on *People Changes*, both recordings featuring Matt Bauder on clarinet.

> *People Changes opens with a cover of Arthur Russell's "A Little Lost" and closes with a cover of Kurt Weisman's "Let My Spirit Rise," the latter featuring Caley Monahon-Ward and recorded after a tour with Weisman and Travis Laplante in 2010.*

On your side of a split LP with Charlie Looker's Extra Life, you include a cover of Spencer Kingman's "Bethlehem-Hell

Express" along with demo versions of "Lifted" and "Weights," released in 2008 on Shatter Your Leaves.

On more recent edits to "Potential Literature," you nearly include Christian Wolff's score for *Stones* alongside Pauline Oliveros' *Rock Piece*, a late addition to the chapter.

Like Beuger's *one tone. rather short. very quiet*, you encounter *Stones* in *Word Events: Perspectives on Verbal Notation*.

> *Make sounds with stones, draw sounds out of stones, using a number of sizes and kinds (and colors); for the most part discreetly; sometimes in rapid sequences. For the most part striking stones with stones, but also stones on other surfaces (inside the open head of a drum, for instance) or other than struck (bowed, for instance, or amplified). Do not break anything.*

The other reference to Wolff appears in "Crippled Symmetry" in relation to Arthur Russell's *City Park*:

> *The only performance of Russell's early work City Park, integrating chamber music, electronics, concrete poetry, turntablism, and modern rock, features composer Christian Wolff on electric bass.*

You initially plan to follow this chapter with a chapter titled "Many Names, Many Faces."

> *Fifty years after its premier, you perform City Park in an ensemble led by University classmate Nick Hallett at the New York City AIDS Memorial on September 30th, 2023.*

The chapter title refers to the original title of the 1st chapter in this text, before it becomes "Combinatory Logics" and then "Language Music," quoting the 1st line from Ann Quin's *Tripticks*.

> *The ensemble features long-time Russell collaborator Peter Zummo, as well as the original drummer in the premier, David Van Tieghem, alongside other University classmates.*

You consider including your recommendation letter from Anthony Braxton redacted in its entirety, with the exception of the phrase—*cosmic radiance*.

> *In your 2nd year at University, Hallett leads an ensemble dedicated to Braxton's vocal music—The Syntactical Ghost Trance Ensemble—of which you are a participant.*

The content consists of the thesis description referenced in the following fragment, a detailed timeline of events displayed in illegible font, and excerpts of answers to the "Intentions, Mysteries, Companions" questionnaire.

As part of the official enrollment procedure for classes in your final year at University, you are asked to write a thesis description for your thesis tutorial, which you initially include here in its entirety, instead of the excerpts below, after abandoning "Many Names, Many Faces."

The above section, between the material appearing in *Sleepingfish* and this fragment, is the last portion of the text that receives extensive revision, calling the work complete on February 15th, 2024.

The above date also marks the day you sign a contract for the book's publication.

In order to expedite the process of signing up and completing your class schedule, you simply write "to create a text of publishable quality," or something of that nature, to which Professor Kuivila responds:

> *The tutorial description is supposed to be the first step in actually writing the thesis, not just a bureaucratic place holder. So I am going to reject the tutorial description and ask you to actually write something that describes your intentions for the thesis.*

You edit your response, using select material written a few months before for the grant proposal, while updating and elaborating on the content as it has evolved accordingly.

On the day you sign the contract, you attend a screening of the film *Deep Listening: The Story of Pauline Oliveros* at University.

Prior to the final revisions of this text occurring in this chapter, your attention is focused primarily on rewriting "Floating Gardens" and expanding "The Story That Most Spends You."

Play is the greatest research tool that the human race has, says Oliveros.

You resubmit the thesis description on September 11th, 2023.

The use of 2nd person narrative creates distance between myself and the content—the "you" in reference implies that there are many versions of myself being referenced (at different points in time) and many versions doing the referencing (the "present" is not stable)—the text acting as a mediator through time, memory, and perception, displaying the multiplicity of self.

You include an edited version of the description to begin the program notes which appear in their entirety in the next chapter.

Another component of the text is to document all of my field recordings, which has become my primary mode of engaging with sound, taking shape around the same time as beginning the composing of the text.

"Many Names, Many Faces" closes with your answer to the final question in "Intentions, Mysteries, Companions," consisting primarily of references to your contextual concert, which takes place on November 28th, 2023, a required performance for 2nd-year graduate students presenting the work of others in context with their own.

I want the writing to reflect the same kind of creativity and exploratory play I've been engaging with in sound.

The concert ends with a reading of excerpts from Gabi Losoncy's *Second Person*, the last page of which appears on the following page, in combination with a field recording of your cat, Tuky, purring in his perch.

Every time you hit a wall, you learn. Every time you do something someone doesn't expect, you learn. The people who write the shape of the thing from the outside will then have to adapt, and if you keep moving so quickly and with increasing definitiveness, even if those moves don't take place in the circumstance of event of physical action, that is a situation that requires recalibration. If you learn to trust your gut, your gut will become better and you will end up doing things you didn't think you were capable of before. There are still lots of things that can be done, and many can be done by you.

Fields: A Contextual Concert

"The more of you there are, the better off we are."

My thesis, Antithesis, attempts to contextualize and synthesize the various threads of creative activity I've pursued over the years across the sonic and literary arts. The text explores a polyphony of overlapping themes that connect and/or contrast with one another, generating something of a disorienting whole. Each sentence is presented as its own distinct fragment, perhaps connecting to the previous or following fragment, or other fragments at varying degrees of distance, and so on, while the use of collage via quotes, scores, program notes, emails and other forms of text aim to constantly reframe and shift the reader's attention. The text itself is its own large-scale composition, engaging with many of the same concepts and formal concerns one might encounter in composing experimental music. One of the primary goals in deviating from the traditional academic research model associated with a conventional thesis is to share my experience in experimental literature with the experimental music community, in hopes to create more dialogue and interactivity across disciplines. The contextual concert program has been carefully considered in an attempt to offer a translation of the text through performance.

INTRODUCTION:
I Went Fishing With My Family When I Was Five *(Tao Lin)*
Rock Piece *(Pauline Oliveros)*

CHAPTER 01:
Combined performances of
Language Music *(Anthony Braxton)*
Autoportrait *(Edouard Levé)*
27 Questions For a Start *(Trio Sowari)*
The Coming Insurrection *(The Invisible Committee)*
Deer Quake *(Aase Berg)*
This Is Not a Novel *(David Markson)*
The Basketball Article *(Bernadette Mayer + Anne Waldman)*
Field *(John Berger)*

CHAPTER 02:
A Little Lost *(Arthur Russell)*
Weights *(Nat Baldwin)*

CHAPTER 03:
Combined performances of
FM *(Nat Baldwin)*
Solo For Wounded CD *(Yasunao Tone)*
Solo For Wounded Solo Contrabass CD *(Nat Baldwin)*
The Maravich Series *("Pistol" Pete Maravich)*

EPILOGUE:
Combined performances of
Second Person *(Gabi Losoncy)*
Untitled 025 *(Nat Baldwin)*

I Went Fishing With My Family When I Was Five — *Tao Lin*
Repetition processes, "alt-lit"-core, a gateway.

Rock Piece — *Pauline Oliveros*
Text score in "Sonic Meditations," non-hierarchical sound-making exercises in listening and responding to an environment.
performed by Lea Bertucci, Sam Boston, Aviva Branoff, Marie Carroll, Marina Diaz, Parsa Ferdowsi, Theodora Fort, Xingjan Guo, Nick Hallett, Emerson Jenisch, Graham Johnson, Nicki Klar, Noa Koffman-Adsit, Zheqin Li, Emma Mistele, Brooks Olson, Shawn O'Sullivan, Arshia Rahmati, Anya Shatilova, Negar Soleymanifar, Xiran Tan, Loren Wang

Language Music — *Anthony Braxton*
Long tones, accented long tones, trills, staccato formings, intervallic formings, multiphonics, short attacks, angular attacks, legato formings, diatonic formings, gradient formings, subidentity formings.
performed by Lea Bertucci, Sam Boston, Marie Carroll, Parsa Ferdowsi, Nick Hallett, Emma Mistele, Shawn O'Sullivan, Michael Pestel, Arshia Rahmati, Negar Soleymanifar

Autoportrait — *Edouard Levé (translated by Lorin Stein)*
Paratactical autofiction with no paragraph breaks, an excerpt from the beginning.
read by Parsa Ferdowsi

27 Questions For a Start — *Trio Sowari (Burkhard Beins, Bertrand Denzler, Phil Durrant)*
Questions generating discourse amongst the so-called "reductionists" in the Berlin improvised music scene in the early to late 00s, published in Echtzeitmusik: Self-Defining a Scene.
read by Sam Boston, Emma Mistele, Arshia Rahmati

The Coming Insurrection — *The Invisible Committee*
Ultra-left political tract by anonymous French collective, an
excerpt from the 1st chapter:"I AM WHAT I AM."
read by Marie Carroll

Deer Quake — *Aase Berg (translated by Johannes Göransson)*
From With Deer, the 1st collection of prose poems by founder of
Stockholm Surrealist Group.
read by Negar Soleymanifar

This Is Not a Novel — *David Markson*
An excerpt from beginning of the ultimate anti-novel novel.
read by Nick Hallett

The Basketball Article — *Bernadette Mayer + Anne Waldman*
A minor masterpiece of conceptual sports writing, a rejected
magazine assignment, an excerpt from the middle.
read by Lea Bertucci

Field — *John Berger*
The 1st 3 paragraphs of the 1st essay in Writing the Field
Recording.
read by Shawn O'Sullivan, Michael Pestel

A Little Lost — *Arthur Russell*
From Another Thought, covered at The Kitchen in 2008 at the
film premier of Wild Combination: A Portrait of Arthur Russell,
opens the 2011 release People Changes.

Weights — *Nat Baldwin*
Composed in 2007, 2nd track on People Changes.

FM — *Nat Baldwin*
Graphic score structured by a series of codes corresponding to actions based primarily on scratching strings with fingernails, composed in November 2002, released on 1st solo album Solo Contrabass the following year while preparing for a return to the court.

Solo For Wounded CD — *Yasunao Tone*
Applying the paramedia tactic of preparing the surface of the CD with pinholes and scotch tape to Solo Contrabass.

Solo For Wounded Solo Contrabass CD — *Nat Baldwin*
A field recording (076) of the wounded Solo Contrabass CD playing through a Sony boombox next to an open window on June 1st, 2023 in Millers Falls, MA. (edited to reduce total time)

The Maravich Series — *"Pistol" Pete Maravich*
Executing and elaborating on a sequence of disciplined actions without amplification and exploring the resonance of surfaces.

Second Person — *Gabi Losoncy*
Excerpts of so-called self-help book from hell by artist working in unaltered, linear audio who makes various decisions with outer consequences based on how she feels, and to the end of expressing how she feels.

Untitled 025 — *Nat Baldwin*
A document of unaltered, linear audio recorded on March 13th, 2023 in Millers Falls, MA.

Field Recordings, Etc

*Field recording, composition and poetic text are three forms
of writing. Each form of writing already involves a kind of
translation. In the broadest sense, a field recording is sound
written by the Earth, or a part of it anyway, on to—or
into—the apparatus of the recorder. The device translates
vibration into electrical impulses that are at some point
translated back into vibration, having undergone a significant change appropriate to the medium of performance or
playback. The composer writes symbols on paper meant to
represent sounds and silences—or at least the potential for
these. This has to be translated by a performer into actual
sound, which will inevitably be different to some degree from
what a composer might have imagined. The written text
also represents sounds that will have to be translated by the
mind of the reader into actual or virtual sound. An image
described in a text is sketched with a degree of abstraction
that asks the reader to fill in the spaces.*

The opening of Michael Pisaro-Liu's essay, above, mentioned in a previous chapter, "Rubies Reddened By Rubies Reddening."

Throughout the process of composing this text, you keep a field recording journal documenting activity as it occurs, marking the date, location, and content in each entry, included here in its entirety following the following fragment.

The entries marked 000, 001, 002, 008, 009 are recorded before the decision to document each recording—000-002 are short sound checks, 008 is a walk through University campus in the snow, and 009 is a less successful version of 010.

> *003-006 — Feb 27th, 2023. Middletown, CTFour tracks of double bass for 8-channel Sound Systems and Chamber Electronics piece. Two tracks recorded with bass on its back. Sounds used: 2-bow tremolo above and below bridge with endpin preparation between fingerboard and strings to dampen open strings, 2-bow tip perc with endpin and left foot damp, 2 wires between endpin and saddle right hand bow with left hand plucks below bridge. Two tracks recorded with bass in its conventional stance. Sounds used: detuned low D interruptions, improvisation centered around spiccato and textural harmonics, slow bow crackles, detuned low D drone, clean harmonics with melodic character.*

> *007 — Feb 28th, 2023. Middletown, CT*
> *Heavy snowfall overnight, walking through University hill filled with snowboarders, skiers, sledders across campus to studio.*

010 — March 1st, 2023. Middletown, CT
Double bass improvisation, recording device sitting on table
slightly below bass bridge. Broken horse hairs drag along
microphones with each bow movement. Action focused on
bridge, strings below bridge, lower bout, purfling, leather
bow quiver tied to tailpiece. EDM on high volume from 2nd
floor, exposed in moments of decreased bass activity.

011-013 — March 4th, 2023. Middletown, CT
Three versions of late night rain: window next to bed, floor
in front of open door with screen shut, floor in front of open
door with screen shut.

014 — March 4th, 2023. Middletown, CT
Making coffee. Materials used: Hario Ceramic Coffee Mill,
Hario Coffee Dripper, Hario V60 Paper Filter, Bonavita
Gooseneck Kettle, 1992 Dream Team mug, Share Coffee
Roasters coffee, water from sink on 2nd floor.

015 — March 4th, 2023. Middletown, CT
Improvisation with bicycle wheel attached to wooden box on
shelf, styrofoam, bubble wrap, shelf, 2 rocks, scissors, 2 bells
next to stairwell picking up student conversation on 2nd floor.

016 — March 5th, 2023. Middletown, CT
Making coffee, attempting to recreate order of actions and
details from previous day's coffeemaking recording from
memory. Materials used: Bonavita Gooseneck Kettle, water
from sink on 2nd floor, 1992 Dream Team mug, Share Coffee
Roasters coffee, Hario Ceramic Coffee Mill, Hario V60 Paper
Filter, Hario Coffee Dripper.

017 — March 6th, 2023. Middletown, CT

Making coffee, attempting to recreate order of actions and details from previous 2 days' coffee-making recording from memory. Materials used: Share Coffee Roasters coffee, water from sink on 2nd floor, Bonavita Gooseneck Kettle, Hario V60 Paper Filter, Hario Coffee Dripper, Hario Ceramic Coffee Mill, 1992 Dream Team mug.

018 — March 7th, 2023. Middletown, CT
Making coffee, attempting to recreate order of actions and details from previous 3 days' coffee-making recording from memory. Materials used: Hario Ceramic Coffee Mill, Share Coffee Roasters coffee, Hario Coffee Dripper, water from sink on second floor, Hario V60 Paper Filter, 1992 Dream Team mug, Bonavita Gooseneck Kettle.

019-024 — March 13th, 2023. Millers Falls, MA
Along Millers River: sitting on a rock; walking toward bridge; directly under bridge; under bridge to left; under bridge to right; walking away from bridge.

025 — March 13th, 2023. Millers Falls, MA
Tuky curled in perch purring.

026 — March 13th, 2023. Turners Falls, MA
Walking along river near Turners Falls-Gill Bridge toward Peskeomskut Island.

027 — March 16th, 2023. Northampton, MA
Walking downtown, bookstore browsing, sitting on bench in Pulaski Park.

028 — March 16th, 2023. Northampton, MA
Reading Give My Regards To Eighth Street by Morton

Feldman at Pulaski Park bus stop.

029 — March 17th, 2023. Millers Falls, MA
Packing Tripticks Tapes orders. Materials used: scissors, scotch tape, bubble wrap, cassettes, padded envelopes, table.

030 — March 17th, 2023. Turners Falls, MA
At post office sending packages referenced in previous entry.

031-033 — March 20th, 2023. Kittery Point, ME
Three recordings at night: fire on rocks near ocean, fire in wood stove in house (short), fire in wood stove in house (long).

034 — March 21st, 2023. Kittery Point, ME
Reading last chapter of Loft Jazz by Michael C. Heller with parents' conversation in next room: a capella practice, ice cream, dog's haircut, dishes, dog.

035 — March 23rd, 2023. Millers Falls, MA
Neighbor conversation on street through open window in apartment: losing power, grilling, tacos, staying out of trouble.

036 — March 23rd, 2023. Millers Falls, MA
Improvisation with triangle waves, pink noise, headphone feedback, open windows, experimenting with approaches for laptop ensemble piece.

037 — March 23rd, 2023. Millers Falls, MA
Train passing, interrupting typing of previous entry.

038-043 — March 24th, 2023. Millers Falls, MA
Six separate tracks following 1st draft of score for laptop

ensemble piece.

044 — March 30th, 2023. Middletown, CT
Walking from Alsop House to University library to check out The San Francisco Tape Music Center: 1960s Counterculture and the Avant-garde edited by David W. Bernstein, Background Noise: Perspectives On Sound Art by Brandon Labelle, MP3: The Meaning of a Format by Jonathan Sterne, Circular Breathing: The Cultural Politics of Jazz In Britain by George McKay, The Other Side of Nowhere: Jazz, Improvisation, and Communities In Dialogue edited by Daniel Fischlin, Keywords In Sound edited by David Novak and Matt Sakakeeny, and The Audible Past: Cultural Origins of Sound Reproduction by Jonathan Sterne.

045 — April 1st, 2023. Middletown, CT
Short improvisation with double bass on ground on its back, recording device placed between bass body and strings with microphones touching strings, experimenting with bow hair crackles and headphone feedback.

046-047 — April 2nd, 2023. Middletown, CT
Two medium-length improvisations with bass and recording device placed in same position as previous fragment. Bow with detached hair used as preparation between strings, 2 other bows used with emphasis on contact with microphones. First pass features more percussive sounds and active attack, 2nd focuses more closely on slow bow movements and detached hair from bow preparation. Both contain various degrees of Twelfth Night by William Shakespeare being rehearsed by student theater group outside building.

048 — April 2nd, 2023. Middletown, CT
Twelfth Night rehearsal with headphone feedback and
detached bow hair contact through open window at Alsop.

049 — April 2nd, 2023. Middletown, CT
Afternoon walk around campus: music studio building
lobby, a capella practice, basement practice studios, outside
admissions office, baseball field, Usdan, admissions tours,
Twelfth Night, Alsop.

050 — April 8th, 2023. Kittery Point, ME
Outside at night in front of Cutts, down path to rocks, back
up to house.

051 — April 9th, 2023. Kittery Point, ME
Experimenting with ideas for solo bass piece, mom vacuuming
and yelling at dog.

052 — April 16th, 2023. Middletown, CT
Reading Experimental Music Since 1970 by Jennie
Gottschalk before bed.

053 — April 19th, 2023. Middletown, CT
Practice with Parsa Ferdowsi and Manny Perez at Alsop.

054 — April 23rd, 2023. New Haven, CT
Performance with Parsa Ferdowsi and Manny Perez at Grey
Matter Books.

055 — April 26th, 2023. Middletown, CT
Electrical transformer box in bushes outside Alsop House.

056 — May 1st, 2023. Middletown, CT

Improvisation with feedback using no-input mixer, a Mackie 1202VLZ4 12-channel, thinking about possibilities for SuperCollider final project for Sound Systems and Chamber Electronics.

057 — May 2nd, 2023. Middletown, CT
Improvisation with feedback using no-input mixer, using same patching and running recording time to exact length of previous night's recording: 43'43".

058 — May 10th, 2023. Middletown, CT
First 2 pieces of Laptop Ensemble concert in WMH from performance position in far back corner of audience. Your piece is 1st, 2nd by Jin Hi Kim. Laptop Ensemble joined by Korean Drumming and Creative Ensemble for Jin Hi Kim's piece.

059 — May 10th, 2023. Middletown, CT
Remainder of Laptop Ensemble concert, shifting position of recording device away from encroaching audience members. Pieces by Sam Boston, James P. Falzone, Parsa Ferdowsi + Zheqin Li, Tobias Haus + Katarina Mazur, Manuel J. Perez III + Y. Alejandra Martinez Rico, and Matthew Evan Taylor.

060-067 — May 12th, 2023. Middletown, CT
Individual pieces for classmates and self at final Sound Systems and Chamber Electronics performance in World Music Hall. Recordings in order of performance: Parsa Ferdowsi, Sam Boston, Jake Manzo, Emerson Jenisch, Daniel Kraft, Nat Baldwin, Sophie Clapacs, Nick Hallett.

068 — May 13th, 2023. Millers Falls, MA

Performance at Audible Bite #1 by Nat Baldwin (double bass) and Victor Signore (saxophones).

069 — May 13th, 2023. Millers Falls, MA
Performance at Audible Bite #1 by Tongue Depressor (Zach Rowden and Henry Birdsey).

070 — May 15th, 2023. Millers Falls, MA
Sitting on porch in morning drinking coffee for 20 minutes.

071 — May 16th, 2023. Millers Falls, MA
Sitting on porch in morning drinking coffee for 20 minutes.

072 — May 18th, 2023. Millers Falls, MA
Sitting in recliner chair in yard in morning drinking coffee. Active birdsong, a slow train passing, neighbors using tools and machines. Planned 20 minutes, clocked 43.

073 — May 25th, 2023. Millers Falls, MA
Sitting on porch in morning drinking coffee, a visit from black cat.

074 — May 31st, 2023. Millers Falls, MA
Train passing overhead, a walk to river and around block.

075 — May 31st, 2023. Millers Falls, MA
Laying in bed, Stella in kitchen listening to Otherppl podcast interview with Scott McClanahan, chopping, cooking.

076 — June 1st, 2023. Millers Falls, MA
First attempts at "Wounded CD" with Solo Contrabass through Sony boombox next to open window in living room.

077 — *June 2nd, 2023. Millers Falls, MA*
Train passing, train stalling, river walk, thunder, train pass ing, rain, running inside, closing windows, Tuky eating, purring, receiving rubs.

078 — *June 2nd, 2023. Millers Falls, MA*
Listening to version of "Wounds/Wounded" on computer, window open, hard rain.

079 — *June 3rd, 2023. Turners Falls, MA*
Performance at The Rendezvous aka The Voo with Victor Signore.

080 — *June 6th, 2023. Millers Falls, MA*
Sitting on porch in morning reading Novels In Three Lines by Félix Fénéon.

081 — *June 7th, 2023. Millers Falls, MA*
Construction on train tracks, standing in driveway, below tracks, both sides of tracks.

082 — *June 8th, 2023. Millers Falls, MA*
Construction on train tracks, standing outside backdoor beneath awning in light rain.

083 — *June 12th, 2023. Northampton, MA*
Reading Novels In Three Lines in Pulaski Park.

084 — *June 12th, 2023. New Haven, CT*
Sweetness the Point of Song (Stella Silbert) at Grey Matter Books.

085 — June 12th, 2023. New Haven, CT
Windscour (Zach Rowden and Joe Moffett) at Grey Matter
Books.

086 — June 12th, 2023. New Haven, CT
Browsing books in between sets at Grey Matter Books,
recording device in bag, buying Muriel Spark's The Prime
of Miss Jean Brodie and Kathy Acker's Great Expectations.

087 — June 12th, 2023. New Haven, CT
Georgia Beatty (fiddle, voice) and Maisie O'Brien (puppets)
at Grey Matter Books.

088 — June 17th, 2023. Millers Falls, MA
Performance at Audible Bite #2 in garage by Liz Tonne
(voice).

089 — June 17th, 2023. Millers Falls, MA
Performance at Audible Bite #2 in garage by Chicken Flag
(Matt Wellins and Max Hamel).

090 — June 20th, 2023. Millers Falls, MA
Dribbling and ball-handling drills in driveway: tapdown,
ball slaps, around waist, cross jog, stance, V side, ricochet,
toss and catch behind, double tap. Train track construction.

091 — June 23rd, 2023. Millers Falls, MA
Day after Brötzmann dies, listening to Machine Gun LP,
recording device in window, train construction.

092 — July 8th, 2023. Millers Falls, MA
Performance at Audible Bite #3 in backyard by poet Zoe Tuck.

093 — July 8th, 2023. Millers Falls, MA
Performance at Audible Bite #3 in backyard by saxophonist
Sam Weinberg.

094 — July 12th, 2023. Millers Falls, MA
Sitting on porch in morning eating yogurt drinking coffee.
Train construction, birds.

095 — July 31st, 2023. Millers Falls, MA
Double bass improvisation, detached-ferrule bow, with
objects: 2 glass funnels, paper, desk.

096 — July 31st, 2023. Millers Falls, MA
Late night: Tuky's perch, open window, blue chair in
kitchen.

097 — August 1st, 2023. Greenfield, MA
Ball-handling/dribbling drills at GHS. Very windy.

098 — August 10th, 2023. Millers Falls, MA
Sitting on porch, woman across street arranging plant
display, building tarp cover, her friend on phone talking
about "Pontiac Club," people passing, planes.

099 — August 10th, 2023. Millers Falls, MA
On couch reading Experimental Music Since 1970 by Jennie
Gottschalk, Stella prepping Audible Bite #4 in kitchen.

100 — August 12th, 2023. Millers Falls, MA
Performance at Audible Bite #4 in backyard by Aisha
Burns.

101 — August 12th, 2023. Millers Falls, MA

Performance at Audible Bite #4 in backyard by Loculus Collective.

102 — August 21st, 2023. Millers Falls, MA
Reading How To Do Nothing by Jenny Odell on porch in morning drinking coffee. One hour and 6 minutes.

103 — August 21st, 2023. Millers Falls, MA
Brushing Tuky at night on living room rug.

104 — August 23rd, 2023. Millers Falls, MA + Erving, MA
River rocks, walk to house, trash cans to garage, landscapers at Bob's, bridge to Erving, train construction, loop to other bridge, across tracks, back to house, porch, plants, Kim. One hour and 26 minutes.

105 — August 26th, 2023. Millers Falls, MA
Listening to Yan Jun Adaptor tape, petting Tuky on couch, scrolling IG (with sound), window open.

106 — August 27th, 2023. Millers Falls, MA
Watching All Together Now by Harry Dodge and Stanya Kahn on couch while Stella makes cake in kitchen.

107-110 — September 2nd, 2023. Millers Falls, MA
Rehearsal with Victor at home.

111 — September 3rd, 2023. Millers Falls, MA
Folding laundry in bedroom, Stella in kitchen making chicken pot pie listening to Maintenance Phase.

112 — September 5th, 2023. Middletown, CT
Practice run of "Species of Spaces" in RHH105, modified for

4 channels.

113 — September 6th, 2023. Brooklyn, NY
Solo set at Roulette, captures "Species of Spaces" and "This
Noise Does Not Stop," but battery runs out at beginning
of "the singing knives."

114-115 — September 9th, 2023. Millers Falls, MA
Audible Bite #5 performance in garage by Webb Crawford.

116 — September 9th, 2023. Millers Falls, MA
Audible Bite #5 performance in garage by Hollow Deck
(Mia Friedman and Andy Allen).

117 — September 9th, 2023. Millers Falls, MA
Audible Bite #5 performance in garage/driveway by Arkm
Foam / Shea Mowat / Donny Shaw.

118 — September 11th, 2023. Millers Falls, MA
Finishing writing description for thesis tutorial request,
updating previous week's recording documentation above,
recording device in window, neighbor construction.

119 — September 14th, 2023. Middletown, CT
Third floor at Alsop: construction/painting parking
lot sidewalk from office window, 2nd floor classroom
conversation from stairwell, South Indian vocal class in
courtyard from back window.

120 — September 21st, 2023. Middletown, CT
Last 10 minutes of 1st Intro to Experimental Music 109
quiz, students passing in papers.

121 — September 21st, 2023. Middletown, CT
Braxton's Language Music "types" demonstration for 109
to send to Paula.

122 — September 24th, 2023. Millers Falls, MA
Packing Tripticks orders, listening to Zhao Cong, Stella
making challah and editing podcast.

123 — October 1st, 2023. Millers Falls, MA
Sitting on porch, late afternoon, reading The Other Name
by Jon Fosse.

124-127 — October 30th, 2023. Millers Falls, MA
First draft realization of The Notecard Quartet score. All
recorded on porch except 1st take.

128 — November 1st, 2023. Middletown, CT
Improvisation with found objects: bicycle wheel attached to
wooden box, styrofoam, bubble wrap, bell, glass cup.

129 — November 1st, 2023. Middletown, CT
Crumpled up bubble wrap uncrumpling.

130 — November 1st, 2023. Middletown, CT
Half bubble wrap noise, half uncrumpling.

131 — November 1st, 2023. Middletown, CT
Headphone feedback, glass cups, styrofoam, bubble wrap.

132 — November 1st, 2023. Middletown, CT
Colbish Circle at Alsop House, Parsa performance (with
audience).

133 — November 1st, 2023. Middletown, CT
Colbish Circle group improvisation.

134 — November 25th, 2023. Millers Falls, MA
Practice read-through of Second Person excerpts along with
025 playing through home speakers, recording device in
front of left speaker.

135 — November 26th, 2023. Middletown, CT
Contextual concert practice in WMH for fixed media/solo
material: Wounded Solo Contrabass CD + Maravich,
Tuky (025) + Second Person.

136-139 — December 4th, 2023. Millers Falls, MA
Updated draft realization for The Notecard Quartet.
Sound material: 2 scissors snipping, paper crumpling,
rubbing together 2 glasses, scratching surface of basketball
with fingernails.

140 — December 10th, 2023. Middletown, CT
Performance of The Notecard Quartet at Crowell Hall
with Marie Carroll, Parsa Ferdowsi, and Loren Wang.

141 — January 1st, 2024. Worcester, MA
Playbackers (Arkm Foam, Donny Shaw, Stella Silbert)
Noise Brunch set at Firehouse.

142 — January 6th, 2024. New York, NY
Sterno at The Stone, 1st show since 2002. Recording device
shuts down around 43 minutes into set, around 20 minutes
before end, front of device reading: "CARD FULL."

The Notecard Quartet

You cut the previous chapter, "First Draft," which provides the foundation for your composition in the 2nd-year Composition Seminar at University, *The Notecard Quartet*.

The composition is to be written for the visiting ensemble, with permission to write oneself into the piece if one desires, which you do.

The visiting ensemble, Ensemble Pamplemousse, will be performing the Seminar participants' pieces the following semester.

Of the 5 ensemble members, Natacha Diels, Andrew Greenwald, and Bryan Jacobs, will be a part of your piece.

The Graduate Composers present prototypes of the compositions with other University students at the end-of-semester concert taking place on December 10th, 2023.

As the concert approaches, you simplify the material articulated in "First Draft," but the basic framework stays the same.

You initially plan to give each performer a notecard filled with numbers that correspond to actions.

A sample notecard given to one performer would look like this:

musical 1 2 3 4
literary 2 3 4 1
quoting 3 4 1 2
personal 4 1 2 3

The numbers in the above example refer to the following actions—*silence (1), text (2), sound (3), open (4).*

If read vertically, each column represents 2 pages, the actions in relation to the categories shifting 4 times throughout the piece.

Each performer would get their own notecard with their own interpretation of the material generated by a new set of numbers.

Since composing the 1st draft, the chapter has been cut from 9 to 7 pages.

You decide that instead of shifting every 2 pages, the actions assigned to each category should stay constant for each individual performer.

The actions are then given new titles—*text* changes to *speak*, *sound* changes to *play*, *silence* changes to *rest*, and *open* changes to *rest* or *speak, off mic*.

You add points of ensemble unity marked by time, an idea encouraged by Natacha Diels, your collaborator/contact person in the ensemble, during a meeting early in the semester.

You provide each participant with scores prepared for performance, taking liberties in your interpretations of the material, limiting the amount of times per page a performer speaks.

The *speak, off mic action* is designed to act as an echo, allowing performers to *speak* a category that is not designated as their primary role.

After listening to a recording of the December concert, you are unsure if the action is necessary, or if it would be more effective in a reduced role, and will likely make some changes before the Pamplemousse performance.

In order to create the scores, you assign the actions to each category for each participant:

notecard 01
musical = speak
literary = rest
quoting = rest / speak, off mic
personal = play

notecard 02
musical = play
literary = speak
quoting = rest
personal = rest / speak, off mic

notecard 03
musical = rest / speak, off mic
literary = play
quoting = speak
personal = rest

notecard 04
musical = rest
literary = rest / speak, off mic
quoting = play
personal = speak

The ensemble in the end-of-semester concert consists of University students Marie Carroll, Parsa Ferdowsi, and Loren Wang, along with yourself.

Each participant is given the following instructions on how to perform their score:

Read through the text, independently of the other performers, interpreting each line through the following corresponding actions:

bold = *speak*
outline = *speak, off mic*
~~line through~~ = *rest*
shadow = *play*

Go slow, rest between each fragment, each page should take around 2'.

Each performer chooses their own sound-making device to use throughout; dynamics are quiet and static, and should stay relatively the same throughout; instrument should require limited movement, in order to focus on reading; ie: found objects, DIY electronics, feedback, small percussion, etc.

3 points of unity + time markings:

end of page 2 = rest 4'-4'30"(interject one brief sound during this time)

end of page 4 = play 8'30"-9'

page 7 = speak (ignore line throughs, repeat last bold fragment until end) 13' -14'

If you arrive early to any of the above, you can begin the action before the indicated time, but be sure to stop on time.

You do not note the detail in the above instructions, but you continue to repeat the last line of the text an additional 4 times after the others stop at the end.

Each performer's role is defined by the category that primarily occupies their speaking parts.

Marie is *notecard 01*, playing the *musical* role, using the crinkling of concert program paper for the play action.

Loren is *notecard 02*, playing the *literary* role, using the scraping together of two bells for the play action.

Parsa is *notecard 03*, playing the *quoting* role, using a stick and the spinning spokes of a wheel affixed to a wooden box for the play action.

You are *notecard 04*, playing the *personal* role, using the rubbing of bubble wrap on the microphone for the play action.

The program notes read as follows:

> *Each performer reads their own distinct interpretation of the same text, created using a formula to evenly distribute actions (rest, speak, play) across 4 major categories of reference (musical, literary, quoting, personal). The text, Language Music, is the 1st chapter of my thesis, Antithesis.*

In the pages following the following fragment, you include the 1st page from *notecards 01*, *02*, and *03*, along with your score for *notecard 04* in its entirety.

The version of the chapter is presented as it appears at the time of performance, before additional edits are applied in preparation for publication.

You are pretty much tempted to quit.

You are weary of pleasing authority.

It should not be a burden, it should be an opportunity, says Professor.

In 2001, applying as a transfer from School of Music, you are denied admittance to University.

Language Music consists of 12 "types" of descriptions offering a basic framework for improvisation.

You nearly attend College instead of School of Music.

Long tones, accented long tones, trills, staccato formings, intervallic formings, multiphonics, short attacks, angular attacks, legato formings, diatonic formings, gradient formings, subidentity formings.

This Is Not A Novel, the second book in David Markson's tetralogy, *The Notecard Quartet,* is published in 2001 by Counterpoint Press.

By combining or moving between "types," one applies *combinatory logics.*

I am trying now an Experiment very frequent among Modern authors; which is, to write upon nothing, says Swift.

The epigraph to *This Is Not a Novel,* above.

Notecard 02

You are pretty much tempted to quit.

You are weary of pleasing authority.

It should not be a burden, it should be an opportunity, says Professor.

In 2001, applying as a transfer from School of Music, you are denied admittance to University.

Language Music consists of 12 "types" of descriptions offering a basic framework for improvisation.

You nearly attend College instead of School of Music.

Long tones, accented long tones, trills, staccato formings, intervallic formings, multiphonics, short attacks, angular attacks, legato formings, diatonic formings, gradient formings, sub- identity formings.

This Is Not A Novel, the second book in David Markson's tetralogy, The Notecard Quartet, is published in 2001 by Counterpoint Press.

By combining or moving between "types," one applies *combinatory logics*.

I am trying now an Experiment very frequent among Modern authors; which is, to write upon nothing, says Swift.

The epigraph to *This Is Not a Novel*, above.

You are pretty much tempted to quit.

You are weary of pleasing authority.

It should not be a burden, it should be an opportunity, says Professor.

In 2001, applying as a transfer from School of Music, you are denied admittance to University.

Language Music consists of 12 "types" of descriptions offering a basic framework for improvisation.

You nearly attend College instead of School of Music.

Long tones, accented long tones, trills, staccato formings, intervallic formings, multiphonics, short attacks, angular attacks, legato formings, diatonic formings, gradient formings, subidentity formings.

This Is Not A Novel, the second book in David Markson's tetralogy, *The Notecard Quartet,* is published in 2001 by Counterpoint Press.

By combining or moving between "types," one applies *combinatory logics.*

I am trying now an Experiment very frequent among Modern authors; which is, to write upon nothing, says Swift.

The epigraph to *This Is Not a Novel*, above.

You are pretty much tempted to quit.

You are weary of pleasing authority.

It should not be a burden, it should be an opportunity, says Professor.

In 2001, applying as a transfer from School of Music, you are denied admittance to University.

Language Music consists of 12 "*types*" of descriptions offering a basic framework for improvisation.

You nearly attend College instead of School of Music.

Long tones, accented long tones, trills, staccato formings, intervallic formings, multiphonics, short attacks, angular attacks, legato formings, diatonic formings, gradient formings, sub-identity formings.

This Is Not A Novel, the second book in David Markson's tetralogy, *The Notecard Quartet*, is published in 2001 by Counterpoint Press.

By combining or moving between "*types*," one applies *combinatory logics*.

I am trying now an Experiment very frequent among Modern authors; which is, to write upon nothing, says Swift.

The epigraph to *This Is Not a Novel*, above.

After an interview with College admissions, you meet with one of the music faculty members, who utters the phrase *"milk and cookies,"* repeatedly.

John Cage's "Lecture On Nothing" is included in *Silence,* his collection of essays and lectures published by Wesleyan University Press.

You have not read Swift.

Before moving near University after receiving rejection, the front passenger side window of your car gets smashed.

It's last day of School of Music and you are moving home for summer, car full of everything you own.

You watch it happen during rehearsal for the concert through a large window in the venue facing the street.

By the time you rush out he's got the whole collection, packed neatly in shoe boxes in the passenger seat.

He acknowledges the Creative Orchestra with a nod before accelerating.

Matthew Welch (soprano, c-soprano, and alto saxophones), Phloyd Starpoli (trombone), Eli Heilbrun (tuba), Nat Baldwin (contrabass), Charlie Looker (electric guitar), Tim Keiper (percussion), Justin Yang (alto, tenor, and baritone saxophones, c-clarinet).

In the fall of 2022, your first semester in the Graduate Program for Experimental Music/Composition, you check out from University library a CD of the concert, which lists the personnel and performance date.

~~*This Is Not A Novel* follows *Reader's Block* and precedes *Vanishing Point* and *The Last Novel*.~~

The narrator, Writer, uses many phrases to describe the text:

~~*an epic poem, a sequence of cantos, a mural of sorts, an autobiography, a continued heap of riddles, a polyphonic opera of a kind, a disquisition on the maladies of the life of art, an ersatz prose alternative to The Waste Land, a contemporary variant on the Egyptian Book of the Dead, an assemblage [non-linear, discontinuous, collage-like], a kind of verbal fugue, his synthetic personal Finnegans Wake, a classic tragedy*~~

Before publication, Markson's *Wittgenstein's Mistress* is reportedly rejected 54 times.

~~David Foster Wallace hails it as a masterpiece – *pretty much the high point for experimental fiction in this country*, blurbs Wallace.~~

~~Ten days after handing in the manuscript for Suicide to his publisher, Edouard Levé dies by suicide at age 42, hanging himself.~~

Jessica delivers the news about the tubist, just over a year after the concert.

~~Levé's other books include *Autoportrait, Newspaper*, and *Works*, as well as three books of photography.~~

The "milk and cookies man," as he refers to himself, Charles Gayle, leaves his teaching position at College, acquired just three years prior, after what would have been your first semester.

In your first semester at School of Music, one professor says: *do not listen to music made past the year 1965.*

You score your 1000th point in the last game of the season, a few months before leaving for School of Music.

Anthony Braxton teaches at University from 1990 to 2013.

For Alto is credited as the first unaccompanied solo saxophone record.

You meet in the hallway as he walks into the venue.

Recorded in 1969, the eight tracks approach nearly 73 minutes in duration, documenting early explorations of *Language Music* and featuring dedications to artists in each track title.

According to the CD you check out from University library, the date is May 21st, 2001.

Jack Gell, John Cage, Murray DePillars, Cecil Taylor, Ann and Peter Allen, Susan Axelrod, Kenny McKenny, Leroy Jenkins.

You have not spoken since the spring of 2002.

The only names familiar to you, outside of their own references in the track listings: *John Cage, Cecil Taylor, Leroy*

Jenkins.

You are familiar with all the names of collaborators with Ishmael Reed.

The epigraph of Flann O'Brien's *At Swim-Two-Birds* quotes Euripedes' *Herakles*.

On August 27th, 1973, Ann Quin walks into the ocean off Palace Pier in Brighton, her body found the next day.

For all things change, making way for each other.

Three months later, her close associate and fellow British literary experimentalist B.S. Johnson slits his wrists in a bathtub.

The Free-Lance Pallbearers, Ishmael Reed's first novel, is published in 1967, and reissued just over three decades later by Dalkey Archive Press.

I have many names. Many faces. At the moment my No. 1 X-wife and and her schoolboy gigolo are following a particularity of flesh attired in a grey suit and button-down Brooks Brothers shirt.

The first three sentences of *Tripticks*, above, Quin's last novel.

Anna Kavan's last novel *Ice* is characterized as "slipstream," a term describing a style of speculative fiction that bends genre and avoids conventional narrative.

Ishmael Reed's texts or lyrics have been performed or set to

music by Albert Ayler, David Murray, Lester Bowie, Don
Pullen, Carla Bley, Olu Dara, Taj Mahal, and Billy Bang,
among others.

Flann O'Brien's given name is Brian O'Nolan.

Born Helen Emily Woods, Kavan originally publishes under
her married name Helen Ferguson before adopting the name
of the protagonist in the two novels she writes just prior to
legally changing her name.

Other pseudonyms used by O'Brien: Myles na gCopaleen,
Brother Barnabas, and George Knowall.

You have not read B.S. Johnson.

A few months later, when you move near University, a
member of Creative Orchestra drops off a stack of burned
CDRs, mostly Braxton, but also Giacinto Scelsi, Jo Kondo,
and Karlheinz Stockhausen.

You first encounter Scelsi through double bassist Joëlle
Léandre and her performance of *Maknongan*, a work for
solo double bass that begins the album *Okanagon*.

You first encounter Cage through Léandre's interpretations
of his work on *The Wonderful Widow of Eighteen Springs*.

Cage's "Ryoanji" is written specifically for Léandre, prompted
by her question to Cage:

Why have you never written anything for double bass?

~~In the liner notes, Léandre provides two words for each letter of the alphabet to describe Cage, along with a short explanation regarding the choices.~~

~~*W* as in wood-block or week-end > **week-end**~~

~~*No point. He worked morning, noon and night. Like Picasso, undoubtedly. Because creating means a perpetual thrust of blood to the temples.*~~

In 2003, Peacock Recordings releases your first solo album, *Solo Contrabass*, right after you stop playing music, a period which lasts about a year.

As composers, our first composition is our life, ~~says Braxton.~~

~~You begin composing this text on February 15th, 2023. The initial working title: *This Is Not a Thesis.*~~

~~You consider composing each fragment on a notecard and collecting them in shoe box tops before assemblage.~~

~~*Nothing more than a fundamentally recognizable genre all the while,* says Markson.~~

Nothing more than a read. *(… repeat until the end)*

Epilogue: A Void

***

A thesis concert by Nat Baldwin on April 16th, 2024

featuring

Lea Bertucci, Sam Boston, Marie Carroll, Parsa Ferdowsi, Nick Hallett, Emma Mistele, Shawn O'Sullivan, Michael Pestel, Arshia Rahmati, Negar Soleymanifar

i. A Void

ii. Fields: Chapter 01

iii. Solo Double Bass (2024)

***

Make an effort to exhaust the subject, even if that seems grotesque, or pointless, or stupid. You still haven't looked at anything, you've merely picked out what you've long ago picked out.
  —*Georges Perec*

What writing music comes down to, in the end, is care. We create situations. We care about them and take care of them. And we care for the people involved.
  —*Michael Pisaro-Liu*

A Void

Chapter 02 in my thesis, Antithesis, is called Potential Literature, titled in reference to the writing group Oulipo, often stylized as OuLiPo, an acronym for Ouvroir de Littérature Potentielle (Workshop for Potential Literature). A Void is a novel by Oulipo member Georges Perec. In the work, he avoids using the most common vowel in the French language throughout the text. I've applied the same technique to the text of Potential Literature as one component of this composition, read by one of the 2 readers. The application in this case, however, occurs after the writing is complete (as opposed to Perec's application of the rule, which guides the composition process), so the effect here is one of subtraction. The other reader applies the inverse strategy and only uses words that contain the vowel. The instrumentalists are also referencing the vowel choices, while the timing of their repeated sound/silent phrases are referencing compositions discussed in the chapter by Antoine Beuger and Manfred Werder. So the compositional strategies in the piece as a whole are essentially a composite drawn from the content of the text. In addition to my own words, there are quotes from John Berger, Antoine Beuger, Wayne Koestenbaum, Edouard Levé, Tom McCarthy, Pauline Oliveros, Georges Perec, Michael Pisaro-Liu, and Raymond Queneau.

with Sam Boston (guitar), Parsa Ferdowsi (text), and Emma Mistele (melodica)

Fields: Chapter 01

With the text in the previous piece referencing parts of my contextual concert, I figured a reprise of one of the pieces from that performance within a new context here would be appropriate. I am particularly excited to present this piece again, as the texts it uses provide a foundation for my thesis, while the collage-like compositional strategies echo the nonlinear, polyvocality of its narrative threads. While the performers are not reading, they'll be guided by Anthony Braxton's Language Music, choosing one "type" to maintain throughout the piece on their instruments. The texts appear as follows, most in excerpted form: Autoportrait by Edouard Levé, translated by Lorin Stein (read by Parsa Ferdowsi), "27 Questions For a Start" by Trio Sowari, from Echtzeitmusik: Self Defining a Scene (read by Sam Boston, Emma Mistele, Arshia Rahmati), The Coming Insurrection by The Invisible Committee (read by Marie Carroll), "Deer Quake" by Aase Berg, from With Deer, translated by Johannes Göransson (read by Negar Soleymanifar), This Is Not a Novel by David Markson (read by Nick Hallett), The Basketball Article by Bernadette Mayer + Anne Waldman (read by Lea Bertucci), and "Field" by John Berger, from Writing the Field Recording (read by Shawn O'Sullivan and Michael Pestel).

Solo Double Bass (2024)

In 2001, I applied to Wesleyan as an undergraduate transfer from the Hartt School of Music. I didn't get in, so I moved to Middletown and audited classes. It was by far the most formative time in my musical development. I had planned to reapply the following year, but instead quit music and went to another school to play basketball. It's a long story, and it's basically where my thesis begins and orbits around, tracing my activity and interests from then until now. During the year that I lived in Middletown, the end of 2001 through 2002, I composed the music that became my 1st solo album, Solo Contrabass. If you were at my contextual concert, the basketball piece with the skipping CD should make more sense now. That earlier era for me at Wesleyan marks the beginning of an ongoing exploration of techniques and concepts that explore all surfaces of the bass as sonic material. In honor of that history, I'm excited to present a new solo piece to close the concert.

Acknowledgements

So much gratitude to my thesis advisor Ron Kuivila, professors and thesis committee members Paula Matthusen and Danielle Vogel, and to all my classmates and collaborators. It's been such a privilege to learn from and alongside so many talented and caring people. I owe so much to the Wesleyan community for supplying a steady source of guidance and light throughout the composition process.

To editors Michael Workman and Meghan Lamb for championing this work with such enthusiasm and dedication throughout the publication process.

To Derek White and Garielle Lutz for publishing "Species of Spaces and Other Pieces" and an excerpt of "Second Person" in *Sleepingfish XX*, and especially to Derek aka Cal A. Mari for the ongoing support.

To Joshua Bohnsack, Cassandra Buell, and Maddalena Kelly for publishing "Language Music" in *Oyez Review,* and to Anna Heflin for publishing "Potential Literature" in *Which Sinfonia.*

To Rita Bullwinkel, Robert Lopez, and Danielle Vogel for offering your astute eyes and ears and for taking the time to compose such thoughtful, generous endorsements.

To Peter Markus and Noy Holland for your mentor/ friendships and for providing initial sparks.

To Micah Silver for your cosmic radiance, for reading early excerpts and consuming all doubt.

To Andre Perry and Mission Creek for your welcoming embrace and well of inspiration.

To Tuky for your warm, calm presence clocking countless writing hours quietly curled by my side.

Extra special thanks to my love Stella Silbert, who I am constantly in awe of and who shared so much encouragement, wisdom, and sweetness throughout this process, while also providing integral pieces of primary source material. She introduced me to *Writing the Field Recording* and *Second Person* and much more. She gifted me *Echtzeitmusik* and *Word Events* and the Zoom H4n Pro Handy Recorder that started me on the path to field recording. Stella's role in this work is immeasurable and I could not have made it without her.

And deepest gratitude to my parents and brother Niles whose unwavering love and support has kept me going through it all, teaching me what it means to truly care.

Endnotes: A Bibliography

Acker, Kathy. *Blood and Guts in High School.* New York: Grove Press, 1978.

Artaud, Antonin. "To Have Done With the Judgement of God." Wave Farm radio art archive. Accessed February 29, 2024. https://wavefarm.org/radio/archive/works/wr8qq5

Badiou, Alain. *Ethics: An Essay on the Understanding of Evil.* Translated by Peter Hallward. London: Verso, 2001.

Baraka, Amiri. *Transbluesency: The Selected Poems of Amiri Baraka/LeRoi Jones (1961-1995).* New York: Marsilio Publishers, 1995.

Baldwin, Nat. *The Red Barn.* New York: Calamari Archive, 2017.

Baldwin, Niles. "Last Page of Books." In *Sleepingfish XX,* edited by Garielle Lutz and Cal A. Mari. New York: Calamari Archive, 2024.

Baumer, Mark. "Crossing America Barefoot: Day 100." January 21, 2017. YouTube video. https://www.youtube.com/watch?v=5O48lxB33k8

Beins, Burkhard. "Labor Diskurs." Translated by William Wheeler. In *Echtzeitmusick Berlin: Self-Defining a Scene*, edited by Burkhard Beins, Christian Kesten, Gisela Nauck, and Andrea Neumann. Hofheim: Wolke Verlag, 2011.

Berg, Aase. *With Deer*. Translated by Johannes Göransson. Boston: Black Ocean, 2009.

Berg, Aase. "Response & Bio." Translated by Johannes Göransson. *Double Room*, Issue #4, Spring/Summer 2004. https://www.webdelsol.com/Double_Room/issue_four/Aase_Berg.html

Berger, John. "Field." In *Writing the Field Recording: Sound, Word, Environment*, edited by Stephen Benson and Will Montgomery. Edinburgh: Edinburgh University Press, 2018.

Beuger, Antoine. "Commentary: *one tone, rather short, very quiet*." In *Word Events: Perspectives on Verbal Notation*, edited by John Lely and James Saunders. London: Continuum, 2012.

Bolaño, Roberto. *By Night in Chile*. Translated by Chris Andrews. New York: New Directions, 2003.

Braxton, Anthony. "Introduction To *Catalog of Works*." In *Audio Culture: Readings in Modern Music*, edited by Christoph Cox and Daniel Warner. Revised edition. New York: Bloomsbury Academic, an imprint of Bloomsbury Publishing Inc, 2017.

Braxton, Anthony. "Trillium E Workshop at Issue Project Room, 2010 June 19." MSS 156, Anthony Braxton Recordings Collection, in the Music Library of Yale University. Accessed February 29, 2024. https://archives.yale.edu/repositories/6/archival_objects/3405706

Cage, John. *Silence: Lectures and Writings*. Middletown, CT: Wesleyan University Press, 1961.

Corbett, John. Liner notes for *The Chicago Octet/Tentet*, Peter Brötzmann. Okka Disk 12022, 1999, 3 compact discs.

Deleuze, Gilles, and Félix Guattari. *A Thousand Plateaus: Capitalism and Schizophrenia*. Translated by Brian Massumi. Minneapolis, MN: University of Minnesota Press, 1987.

Elkin, Lauren, and Veronica Esposito. "An Attempt at Exhausting a Movement." *The New Inquiry*, January 13, 2013. https://thenewinquiry.com/an-attempt-at-exhausting-a-movement/

Endnotes. "About *Endnotes*." Accessed February 29, 2024. https://endnotes.org.uk/pages/about

Evenson, Brian. *Altmann's Tongue: Stories and a Novella*. Lincoln, NE: Bison Books, 2002.

Gladman, Renee. *Event Factory*. 1st ed. Urbana, IL: Dorothy, a publishing project, 2010.

Grundy, David. "Everything That You Do: On the Poetry of Cecil Taylor." *Chicago Review*, February 3, 2020. https://www.chicagoreview.org/david-grundy-everything-that-you-do-onthe-poetry-of-cecil-taylor/

Grundy, David. "…And Not Goodbye: Cecil Taylor As Poet." *Streams of Expression*, April 29, 2018. http://streamsofexpression.blogspot.com/2018/04/and-not-goodbye-cecil-taylorpart-2.html

Haenisch, Matthias. "About Polwechsel." Accessed February 29, 2024. http://www.polwechsel.com/inde.htm

Heller, Michael C. *Loft Jazz : Improvising New York in the 1970s*. Oakland, CA: University of California Press, 2017.

Holland, Noy. *Swim for the Little One First*. Tuscaloosa,

AL: FC2, 2012.

Howard, Joanna. *Rerun Era, or, The Dislocations*. San Francisco: McSweeney's, 2019.

The Invisible Committee. *The Coming Insurrection*. Los Angeles: Semiotext(e), 2009.

Johnston, John. Introduction to "In the Shadow of the Red Brigades" by Sylvère Lotringer. In *Autonomia: Post-Political Politics*, edited by Hedi El Kholti, Sylvère Lotringer, and Christian Marazzi. 2nd ed. / prepared by Hedi El Kholti. Los Angeles: Semiotext(e), 2007.

Kowald, Peter. Liner notes in *Was Da Ist*, Peter Kowald. FMP 62, 1994, compact disc.

Koestenbaum, Wayne. "The Prince of Parataxis: Édouard Levé's Visionary Book of Unrelated Ideas." *Bookforum*, Apr/May 2012. https://www.bookforum.com/print/1901/edouard-leve-svisionary-book-of-unrelated-ideas-9165

Léandre, Joëlle. Liner notes in *The Wonderful Widow of Eighteen Springs* by John Cage, Joëlle Léandre. Montaigne 782121, 2004, compact disc.

Levé, Edouard. *Autoportrait*. Translated by Lorin Stein. 1st ed. Champaign, IL: Dalkey Archive Press, 2012.

Levé, Edouard. "When I Look at a Strawberry, I Think of a Tongue." Translated by Lorin Stein. *The Paris Review*, Issue 196, Spring 2011. https://www.theparisreview.org/letters-essays/6078/when-i-look-at-a-strawberry-i-think-of-a-tongue-edouard-leve

Lispector, Clarice. *The Hour of the Star*. Translated by Benjamin Moser. New York: New Directions, 2011.

Lispector, Clarice. *The Passion According to G.H*. Translated by Idra Novey. New York: New Directions, 2012.

Losoncy, Gabi. *Second Person*. Austin, TX: Amphetamine Sulphate, 2017.

Markson, David. *This Is Not a Novel*. Washington, D.C: Counterpoint, 2001.

Markson, David. *Wittgenstein's Mistress*. 1st ed. Elmwood Park, IL: Dalkey Archive Press, 1988.

Mayer, Bernadette, and Anne Waldman. *The Basketball Article*. Los Angeles: Franchise, 2021.

Moten, Fred. *In the Break: The Aesthetics of the Black Radical Tradition*. Minneapolis, MN: University of Minnesota Press, 2003.

Nakamura, Toshimaru. "Toshimaru Nakamura Sound Student." Interview by William Meyer. *Perfect Sound Forever*, 2003. https://www.furious.com/perfect/toshimarunakamura.html

O'Brien, Ellen. "Coach Denies Player's Charge." *Boston Globe*, November 5, 1998.

O'Brien, Flann. *At Swim-Two-Birds*. Normal, IL: Dalkey Archive Press, 1998.

Oliveros, Pauline. "Rock Piece." In *Flint Magazine*, Issue 1+2, 2018. https://sensatejournal.com/pauline-oliveros-rock-piece/

Oliveros, Pauline. *Deep Listening: The Story of Pauline Oliveros*, directed by Daniel Weintraub. Accord, NY: Capone Productions, 2022.

Panzner, Joe. *The Process That Is the World: Cage/Deleuze/Events/Performances*. New York: Bloomsbury Academic, 2017.

Parker, William. Liner notes in *Through Acceptance of the Mystery Peace*, William Parker. Eremite Records MTE012, 1998, compact disc.

Pisaro-Liu, Michael. "Rubies Reddened By Rubies Reddening." In *Writing the Field Recording: Sound, Word,*

Environment, edited by Stephen Benson and Will Montgomery. Edinburgh: Edinburgh University Press, 2018.

Pisaro-Liu, Michael. "Writing, Music." *In The Ashgate Research Companion to Experimental Music*, edited by James Saunders. Farnham, UK: Ashgate, 2009.

Perec, Georges. *Species of Spaces and Other Pieces.* Translated by John Sturrock. London: Penguin Books, 1997.

Perec, Georges. *A Void.* Translated by Gilbert Adair. London: Harvill Press, 1995.

Queneau, Raymond. *Exercises In Style.* Translated by Barbara Wright. New York: New Directions, 1981.

Quin, Ann. *Three.* Normal, IL: Dalkey Archive Press, 2001.

Quin, Ann. *Tripticks.* Normal, IL: Dalkey Archive Press, 2002.

Rainey, Bhob. "Introduction." In *The BSC Manual*, edited by Bhob Rainey. New Orleans, LA: NO Books, 2011.

Reed, Ishamel. *The Free-Lance Pallbearers.* Normal, IL: Dalkey Archive Press, 1999.

Sachiko M. "The Queen of the Sine Wave Kingdom Explains Herself." Interview by Takashi Azumaya. Translated by Cathy Fishman. *Improvised Music From Japan 2002-2003*, launch issue: p. 12-14.

Sachiko M. "Off Site: Improvised Music From Japan," quoted by Clive Bell, October 24, 2014, https://daily.redbullmusicacademy.com/2014/10/off-site-improvised-music-from-japan

Shepp, Archie. "Black Music Survived Not Because But In Spite of Capitalism." In *Free Jazz Communism: Archie Shepp-Bill Dixon Quartet at the 8th World Festival of Youth and Students in Helsinki 1962*, edited by

Sezgin Boynik and Taneli Viitahuhta. Helsinki: Rab-Rab Press, 2020.

Shepp, Archie. "I Will Not Let You Misconstrue Me." In *Free Jazz Communism: Archie Shepp–Bill Dixon Quartet at the 8th World Festival of Youth and Students in Helsinki 1962*, edited by Sezgin Boynik and Taneli Viitahuhta. Helsinki: Rab-Rab Press, 2020.

Taylor, Cecil. Liner notes in *Indent*, Cecil Taylor. Freedom FR 11008, 1977, LP.

Taylor, Cecil. *Imagine the Sound*, directed by Ron Mann. San Francisco: Kanopy Streaming, 2015.

Tiqqun. *This Is Not a Program*. Translated by Joshua David Jordan. Los Angeles: Semiotext(e), 2011.

Weiss, Jason. *Always in Trouble: An Oral History of ESP-Disk, the Most Outrageous Record Label in America*. Middletown, CT: Wesleyan University Press, 2012.

Wilmer, Valerie. *As Serious As Your Life: Black Music and the Free Jazz Revolution, 1957-1977*. London: Serpent's Tail, 2018.

Wolff, Chritian. "Stones (1968)." In *Word Events: Perspectives on Verbal Notation*, edited by John Lely and James Saunders. London: Continuum, 2012.

Yoshida, Ami. "Let's Talk: About Ami Yoshida." Interview by Minoru Hatanaki. *Improvised Music From Japan EXTRA 2003*: p. 38-40.

Yoshihide, Otomo. "Anode Note." Translated by Toshimaru Nakamura. *Improvised Music From Japan 2002-2003,* launch issue: p. 16-17.

Nat Baldwin is a double bassist, composer, and writer from Maine currently living in Western Massachusetts. He's released several solo and collaborative works across genres and runs the experimental music label Tripticks Tapes. His books include a collection of short fiction, *The Red Barn* (Calamari Archive, 2017), and a work of hybrid nonfiction, *Antithesis* (Bridge Books, 2025).

A selection of field recordings and compositions featured within these pages can be found at infra-ordinaryarchive.bandcamp.com